PORTFOLIO / PENGUIN

MASTERING THE VC GAME

Jeffrey Bussgang, a successful serial entrepreneur for ten years, is now a general partner at Flybridge Capital Partners, an early-stage venture capital firm with more than $500 million under management. Before becoming a venture capitalist, he was the cofounder of Upromise, the largest private source of college funding contributions in the United States. He also serves as an entrepreneur in residence at Harvard Business School, where he earned an MBA with highest distinction. Bussgang writes a popular blog, www.SeeingBothSides.com, and lives in the Boston area with his wife and three children.

MASTERING THE VC GAME

A Venture Capital Insider
Reveals How to Get
FROM START-UP TO IPO
on **YOUR** Terms

JEFFREY BUSSGANG

PORTFOLIO / PENGUIN

To my parents, who created me,

and my wife, who sustains me

PORTFOLIO/PENGUIN
Published by the Penguin Group
Penguin Group (USA) Inc., 375 Hudson Street,
New York, New York 10014, U.S.A.
Penguin Group (Canada), 90 Eglinton Avenue East, Suite 700,
Toronto, Ontario, Canada M4P 2Y3
(a division of Pearson Penguin Canada Inc.)
Penguin Books Ltd, 80 Strand, London WC2R ORL, England
Penguin Ireland, 25 St. Stephen's Green, Dublin 2, Ireland
(a division of Penguin Books Ltd)
Penguin Books Australia Ltd, 250 Camberwell Road, Camberwell,
Victoria 3124, Australia
(a division of Pearson Australia Group Pty Ltd)
Penguin Books India Pvt Ltd, 11 Community Centre, Panchsheel Park,
New Delhi – 110 017, India
Penguin Group (NZ), 67 Apollo Drive, Rosedale, Auckland 0632,
New Zealand (a division of Pearson New Zealand Ltd)
Penguin Books (South Africa) (Pty) Ltd, 24 Sturdee Avenue,
Rosebank, Johannesburg 2196, South Africa

Penguin Books Ltd, Registered Offices: 80 Strand, London WC2R ORL, England

First published in the United States of America by Portfolio, a member of
Penguin Group (USA) Inc. 2010
This paperback edition with a new preface published 2011

THE LIBRARY OF CONGRESS HAS CATALOGED
THE HARDCOVER EDITION AS FOLLOWS:
Bussgang, Jeffrey.
Mastering the VC game : a venture capital insider reveals how to get from
start-up to IPO on your own terms / Jeffrey Bussgang.
p. cm.
Includes index.
ISBN 978-1-59184-325-2 (hc.)
ISBN 978-1-59184-444-0 (pbk.)
1.Venture capital.   2.New business enterprises—Finance.   3.Going public (Securities)   I. Title.
HG4751.B875   2010
658.15'224—dc22   2009053945

Printed in the United States of America
Set in Stempel Garamond
Designed by Victoria Hartman

CONTENTS

PREFACE

Since the publication of *Mastering the VC Game* in 2010 I
have received wonderful feedback from the entrepreneurial
community. In fact, I have been blown away by the response
from such a diverse population of entrepreneurs and would-be
entrepreneurs around the world. One twenty-something entrepreneur working at a non-profit in Australia wrote me:

> Thank you for writing this book. It was a captivat-
> ing read that gave me the basics of how the industry
> looks. I loved it. My only problem was feeling inspired
> to action, which made me put the book down to send
> emails to friends and look up companies, which was a
> great problem to have.

Inspiring entrepreneurs into action was my original goal
for the book. Now, as the global economic crisis recedes in

the rear view mirror, both policy makers and business leaders have come to recognize that the capacity of human beings to innovate is our best hope for addressing and ultimately solving society's thorniest problems. It has never been more critical that we brew up that magic elixir that comes from mixing entrepreneurs, who are the source of innovation, with investors, who are the source of capital to fuel that innovation. I wrote *Mastering the VC Game* to inspire, in some small way, entrepreneurs around the world to arm themselves with the knowledge, skills, and tools they need to take action and to succeed in their endeavors and attract the necessary funds to accelerate their vision.

It turns out that I was fortunate in the choice of companies and founders profiled here. When I began writing, four of them—Baidu, LinkedIn, Twitter, and Zynga—were relative unknowns outside the insular start-up community, but have since become household names with multi-billion-dollar valuations. Their success further validates the lessons included in the book, although there is also much to be learned from the failures that those early founders suffered (and openly discuss here).

Since publication, a few significant trends have emerged. One of the most important has been the rise of angel investors as an influential source of capital for entrepreneurs. This has come about through the confluence of two forces: the rapid reduction in costs required for a lean start-up to initiate operations and achieve early success—thanks to cheaper infrastructure, cloud computing, social media marketing, and more sophisticated techniques for getting initial customer feedback; and the return into the start-up ecosystem of dollars and talent from successful entrepreneurs at start-up companies like Google, Paypal, and others.

Interestingly, these developments have been disruptive to many early-stage venture capital investors who have focused on consumer Internet and mobile start-ups, particularly in Silicon Valley. Many VCs find themselves competing with their former entrepreneur friends who have made enough money that they can afford to invest in young start-ups themselves. In response, VCs have adjusted their model by participating alongside angels in "seed" rounds that are often less than $1 million or focusing on later stage investing. Further, successful angels have attracted enough interest and capital that they have become more institutionalized (earning the nickname "super angels") or raised outside capital and hired young associates to scale their model into something that looks remarkably like a small VC fund. Entrepreneurs that can successfully navigate this new landscape have more funding choices than ever, especially at the earliest stages when they seek only a modest amount of capital. By and large, I believe that it's a good thing for us all that entrepreneurs have these new options from which to choose.

We have witnessed some important new technological trends in the past few years, particularly the launch of the iPad and tablet computing, the continuing explosion of smart phones and applications, and a massive cost reduction in the mapping of the human genome, which has the potential to change the game in health care and a broad range of industrial fields. Not surprisingly, most of the companies leading the way in these exciting areas are VC-backed.

These trends and others like them have further fueled the need for the kind of cooperation between VCs and entrepreneurs I describe in the book. When entrepreneurs and investors align and work in harmony, the long odds for start-up success are greatly improved and real magic can happen. If you can master the VC game, you might be the one to create the next Google, Facebook, or Twitter!

Happy reading and good luck.

Best,
Jeff Bussgang

P.S. Visit my blog to keep the dialogue going—www.Seeing BothSides.com.

MASTERING
THE VC GAME

INTRODUCTION

I was born to be an entrepreneur. Becoming a venture capitalist (VC) was never part of my life plan.

Reid Hoffman, founder of LinkedIn, observed that an entrepreneur is someone who will jump off a cliff and assemble an airplane on the way down. This is certainly an impulse to which I can relate. I credit my father with sparking my entrepreneurial drive. He was a Holocaust refugee and survivor, who came to America, penniless, in 1949 and earned his master's in engineering from MIT and PhD in applied physics from Harvard. He then started a successful high-technology company the old-fashioned way—living hand to mouth, operating with customer revenues only, and without benefit of any outside capital. Watching my immigrant father embrace entrepreneurship inspired in me a passion for the field and an unyielding belief in its power to effect change.

Armed with a "kitchen table" MBA, as well as the real thing from Harvard Business School, I set out many years ago on my own entrepreneurial journey. During the ten years I spent making my way as an entrepreneur and executive team member of two venture-backed start-ups—Upromise (which I co-founded in 2000) and Open Market (IPO 1996)—I interacted with and pitched to many VCs and became fascinated with the VC game. So, after a decade of scratching the entrepreneurial itch, I went over to the "other side" and became a VC myself. I joined a new VC firm, called Flybridge Capital Partners, that a couple of friends had just started.

I initially both revered and feared VCs as powerful, intimidating characters in possession of the one thing entrepreneurs are desperate to get access to: capital. As I spent more time with VCs as my partners and co-investors, I learned what made them tick and how entrepreneurs can be most effective in pitching to them, managing a VC-led board of directors, and successfully navigating an exit.

I wrote this book to demystify the VC world for entrepreneurs, having seen both sides as an insider, and to help entrepreneurs level the playing field when pursuing venture capital so that they can secure the resources necessary to achieve their vision. In this book, I reveal industry insights drawn from my experience as a practicing VC. I also include the perspectives of partners from some of the leading VC firms around the world who were kind enough to divulge their own secrets about their approach to the business.

I was also fortunate enough to be able to convince some of today's most successful entrepreneurs—including the founders of Constant Contact, LinkedIn, Sirtris, Twitter, Zynga, and others—to talk from their deep knowledge and experience about how to work with VCs to shape a young company and help it grow. The purpose of this book is to share the magic formula of how great entrepreneurs team with VCs to create valuable companies from raw start-up. Whether you are the next Mark Zuckerberg (the Harvard student who started Facebook) or Jim Barksdale (the seasoned Fortune 500 executive who became CEO of Netscape), *Mastering the VC Game* will provide you with an insider's guide to the world of VC-backed company formation, growth, and exit.

In the book's first two chapters, I will explore the psyche of the two protagonists in the start-up game: the entrepreneur and the VC. In Chapters 3 and 4, I turn to the process of raising money ("the pitch") and negotiating the deal. Chapters 5 and 6 provide insight into the company-building process and the way entrepreneurs and VCs make money by selling their companies ("the exit"). After a profile of the VC business outside the United States in Chapter 7, I conclude with a few observations about the industry's future direction.

I have written this book not only to share this knowledge so that others can pursue their dreams—and, if things go well, turn their investments into handsome returns—but also because I strongly believe in the positive impact the venture-backed start-up can have on our economy and our society as a whole.

VCs acting in concert with entrepreneurs function as an essential and powerful engine of the U.S. economy. In the more than forty years since the very first venture-backed start-up—Digital Equipment Corporation (DEC), which was founded by Ken Olsen with a $70,000 investment in 1959 and went public in 1968 with a market value of $37 million, a 528-fold return!—VCs have invested more than $450 billion in some 57,000 companies in the United States. More than 12 million people (about 12 percent of the U.S. workforce) now hold jobs and make careers at venture-backed companies, and those businesses have combined sales of $2.9 trillion or over 20 percent of the total business revenues in the United States. And the VC game has led to the creation of some of the most iconic of American companies: Amazon, Apple, eBay, Facebook, Google, Intel, LinkedIn, Microsoft, Staples, Starbucks, Twitter, and YouTube.

The venture-capital-driven entrepreneurship model has also become one of America's most influential and important exports. Increasingly, the venture-backed start-up is becoming a key driver of growth and innovation in countries around the world. In the rapidly developing countries, venture capital investment is spreading like wildfire—up from zero just a few years ago to $4 billion in China and nearly $1 billion in India in 2010, and those numbers are expected to grow rapidly in the next few years.

Both in the United States and abroad, the venture-backed start-up plays an important role beyond innovation and wealth creation: changing the world for the better. Entrepreneurs and VCs alike invest in dreams—from new sources of energy to curing cancer to revolutionizing education—that have the potential to benefit society as well as themselves. Although the majority of entrepreneurs do *not* go the VC route to raise money to fuel their businesses, for many reasons that we'll discuss, all can benefit from learning how the VC-backed start-up formula works.

Over the next decade, hundreds of billions of dollars will be invested in new or young companies and it is critical that this capital be invested wisely. With the accelerating development of technology, widespread digitalization, broadband Internet, wireless devices and communications, environmental and energy breakthroughs, and medical advancements, the stakes are getting higher and the potential for world-changing opportunities is greater than ever before. *Mastering the VC Game* will help entrepreneurs be more effective in financing and launching start-ups and in creating companies that benefit us all, while also providing insight into the critical role these enterprises play in the global economy.

THE ENTREPRENEURIAL ITCH:
CHANGE THE WORLD

To truly understand the world of VC-backed start-ups, it is necessary to first delve into the psyche of the entrepreneur, because it is fundamentally different from that of the conventional businessperson.

I have had the entrepreneurial drive for as long as I can remember. I was fascinated by technology as a kid. I tease my parents that my love for computers originates from all the video games I played while hanging around ice rinks waiting for my older sister, then a competitive ice-skater, to finish practice. When the Apple II came out, I begged my parents to buy one for me, and I gladly invested the earnings from my paper route in the purchase.

I got my first crack at working in a start-up during the summer of my first year in business school. I became a member of the "executive team" of a software start-up. The entire staff of ten worked out of an apartment in Boston, located in an alley behind a Chinese restaurant. I can still remember the smell—and not fondly. The vice president of marketing usually brought her dog to the "office," and she (the dog, that is) always seemed to bark loudly when I was just about to close a deal on the phone.

This first start-up experience proved to be great fun. It was a sandbox where I learned about the real-world pressures of operating a small software company: shipping products, working with partners, meeting payroll, and doing deals.

From that first experience of the entrepreneurial life, I was hooked.

The nature of the entrepreneur hasn't changed much, if at all, since I was a student. This is very evident at a networking event that our firm, Flybridge Capital Partners, holds every year for graduating students of Harvard Business School and MIT Sloan School of Management. We invite dozens of young men and women who are thinking about becoming entrepreneurs.

What always strikes me about the event is that the students seem almost completely unaffected by the economic ups and downs raging around them. For example, in 2009—one of the worst years for the economy in decades—they were unfazed by the collapse of the credit markets, the destruction of trillions in stock market and real estate value, and global recession. In fact, those topics didn't even come up.

No, they wanted to talk about clean technology and sustainability, the rise of Facebook, novel medical devices and sensors, Google versus Microsoft, the opportunities represented by the emerging mobile generation, and the shift of the hundreds of billions of dollars in global advertising to the Web. Many were focused on opportunities in developing countries, the emergence of a global perspective on venture capitalism and entrepreneurship, and all kinds of other fascinating topics.

In short, what continued to drive them was the entrepreneurial itch. Yes, they were concerned about landing a job somewhere after graduation in a few short months, but they were much more focused on ideas, innovations, and opportunities. It is no coincidence that the MIT $100,000 business plan competition, and dozens like it around the country, has a steadily growing number of entrants each year. Student-led entrepreneurial teams clamor to submit business plans in the hopes of winning a little seed money and a lot of notoriety.

I can only conclude that, in the minds of the graduates of American business schools, it is always "morning in America" (thank you, Ronald Reagan) and that our entrepreneurial economy is forever a city on a shining hill (thank you, John Winthrop), even when there is economic upheaval. In fact, now more than ever, the entrepreneurial economy is an appealing destination for top talent around the world.

IT'S NOT (PRIMARILY) ABOUT THE MONEY

One thing you do not hear these graduates talk about, at least not directly, is the money. Of course, they want to make money—and being optimists, they assume they will—but that is never their focus.

I completely identify with this point of view. As a kid, when listening to my parents discuss the work of my father's company, I was surprised that they talked mostly about people and relationships rather than technology and money. How could the vice president of engineering communicate better with the vice president of marketing? Is the technical team getting along as well as they should on the new project? It was then that I learned the centrality of human relations in business, a theme that has guided my career and a theme that plays out over and over again in this book in the stories of the entrepreneurs and VCs that I interviewed.

That influence is probably why I made decisions to prioritize pursuing my intellectual interests over money, especially early in my career, preferring instead to focus on the thrill of playing the entrepreneurial game. The first time was in early 1995, not long before I graduated from HBS. I was invited to dinner with several members of a prestigious Boston-based venture capital firm. The dinner went well and the partners asked me to fly to Silicon Valley and meet with some other members of the firm. Long story short, I received an offer to join the firm.

I had been so focused on becoming an entrepreneur, however, that I didn't know how to evaluate the opportunity. I didn't even really know what the VC industry was all about and how it worked. I consulted with some friends, and they told me to consider two factors. First, the money. They said that senior partners at top-tier VC firms earn a staggering amount of money over the course of a long, successful career (one of my friends referred to the VC world as a "get rich slow business"). Second, the nature of the work itself. As one of the firm's partners put it, the work was "a mile wide and an inch deep." You could work across many different arenas but never get to dig in and actually build something of your own.

Tempting, but after some soul-searching, I decided I preferred to follow my passion for entrepreneurship. I concluded that I didn't care about the raw economics of the opportunity as much as the nature of the opportunity. I *wanted* to get my hands dirty and build new products and lead teams. So I declined the offer, expecting that would be the end of the relationship with the VCs.

Not so. They graciously offered to introduce me to a few of their portfolio companies. One of them was Open Market, a Boston-area Internet start-up whose mission was to develop the infrastructure software that would help turn the Internet into a safe business environment—exactly my area of interest. I jumped at the chance to join the company as an entry-level product manager with a salary of $65,000 a year, more money than I had ever made, but still a fraction of the average starting salary for a Harvard MBA at the time.

My classmates thought I was crazy, but I couldn't resist the allure of a start-up—it was simply in my blood.

Fortunately, my instincts proved right.

Open Market was an incredibly exciting company. We hired two hundred people in the year after I arrived and quickly grew to over five hundred employees. I was fortunate to rise swiftly through the ranks and soon joined the executive team. Twelve months after I came aboard, the company went public. Although we had just $1.8 million in revenue, we achieved a market capitalization (total value of all outstanding stock) of over $1 billion. At age twenty-six, I had become a paper millionaire. More important, to me anyway, I had learned a lot and had a tremendous ride.

But like all addicted entrepreneurs, I wanted more. I wanted another ride.

THE SIREN SONG OF SERENDIPITY

I have a strong belief in the power of random connections—the siren song of serendipity. I have always admired the way successful entrepreneurs put themselves in a position to "get lucky" by developing relationships with relevant people and taking advantage of promising opportunities. So, in 1999, while still at Open Market, I accepted, for no particular reason, an invitation to meet with Michael Bronner, one of Boston's most successful entrepreneurs (founder of the leading interactive marketing firm Digitas). Michael wanted to start a company that would help parents set aside money for college tuition and also enable large consumer companies to create strong customer relationships through loyalty programs.

Over breakfast, Michael described the idea in great detail and the unique culture we could create by building a company that would do well by doing good. I have to confess that he had me at "hello."

It wasn't that I wanted out of Open Market. I was perfectly happy there. Once again, however, the siren call of starting a new venture and the appeal of the mission were so strong that I decided to pursue my passion and joined Michael to help start the new company, becoming its founding president.

We called the company Upromise.

We initially worked out of Michael's house in a suburb of Boston and made plans for global domination. We hired twenty people in the first three months of the venture and rapidly built out our team and infrastructure. The technical team began developing software in the spare bedroom. The living room was taken over by marketing and the dining room by business development. When the trucks and crews rolled through this exclusive neighborhood, hauling computer equipment or installing high-speed lines, we became very unpopular neighbors. First, the speed bumps arrived. Then, a town zoning inspector paid a visit. Eventually, we were chased out of Michael's house and had to find proper office space.

In our first year, we raised nearly $100 million in two rounds of financing from several blue-chip venture capital firms, hired fifty more employees, and signed a flurry of business partnerships. After many twists and turns, including surviving the bursting of the technology bubble, Upromise became a successful company. Sallie Mae acquired it in 2006, a few years after I had left, and by 2011, the firm administered $35 billion in college savings plans and had 12 million households using the service.

AN ENTREPRENEUR'S MAKEUP

Although I spent the first ten years of my professional life as an entrepreneur, I didn't fully understand the entrepreneur's mind-set—my own mind-set, that is—until I went to the other side and became a venture capitalist. (More on how *that* happened in the next chapter.)

As I listened to pitch after pitch and watched as some venture-backed start-ups took off and others didn't, I became much more aware that the successful entrepreneur is built, in fact, *has* to be built, in ways that are fundamentally different from other businesspeople.

Many start-up entrepreneurs would simply hate being a

big company executive. The conventional wisdom is that they just don't have the management skills necessary to run a large company. Although it's true that most entrepreneurs could not successfully manage thousands or even tens of thousands of people in a complex organization, there are exceptions. Bill Gates is the best example of a brilliant entrepreneur who has succeeded along the whole arc—starting from scratch to leading one of the world's largest and most important companies.

I think the difficulty that start-up executives have in fitting in comfortably into a big company is more about what drives an entrepreneur and what satisfies him or her—both in the long run and in the day-to-day work. It comes down to an essential character trait that I observed in myself: the entrepreneurial itch. When you have it, you just have to scratch it. You really can't help yourself.

Being an entrepreneur may be something deep in the genes. John Doerr, the venture capitalist, described some of the greatest entrepreneurs he had invested in—including Sergey Brin and Larry Page (Google), Jeff Bezos (Amazon.com), and Steve Jobs (Apple)—as "geeks who couldn't get dates." Although I don't know if that is actually true about those four guys, the spirit of the comment resonates. The world of the entrepreneur, even when they are teenagers, is typically not defined by being cool and fitting in but rather by their passion for technology, innovation, change, and a particular idea.

Genetic or not, there are certain classic characteristics of the entrepreneur. The most important of these are a certain kind of visionary optimism; tremendous confidence in oneself that can inspire confidence in others; huge passion for an idea or phenomenon that drives them forward; and a desire to change the game, so much so that it changes the world. Below I'll introduce three entrepreneurs (Flybridge is not an investor in any of them) that fit this model. They may not be household names like Bezos and Jobs, but each of their companies is well on its way: Sirtris, Twitter, and LinkedIn.

VISIONARY, PASSIONATE OPTIMIST:
A DRUG THAT KEEPS YOU YOUNG

Entrepreneurs tend to genuinely believe that their brilliant vision can make the world a better place. What else would you expect from a person who works—typically day and night and often for a relatively low salary—to create something that does not exist and for which there is not even a model? If the entrepreneur isn't optimistic, isn't a true believer in his own vision, who will be?

However, I've found that although the entrepreneur displays these positive traits to the outside world, more negative concerns may also be driving him. For example, the entrepreneur's incredible optimism that everything will go right is often accompanied by a raging fear that, in fact, everything will go totally wrong. Strangely, many venture capitalists respect and respond as much to the paranoia as they do to the optimism, perhaps because they, too, can be ambivalent in their outlook.

Take, for example, Dr. Christoph Westphal. Here's his audacious belief: that his company, Sirtris Phar-

Christoph Westphal

maceuticals, can create a drug that will keep you thin and help you live forever—well, at least for a substantially longer time, perhaps ten or twenty years, than you would live without the drug.

Of course, that's not exactly how Sirtris describes its product. The company's research focuses on developing drugs to target enzymes called sirtuins, including resveratrol, a naturally occurring compound found in the skin of red grapes (as well as in many plants). When activated, these enzymes produce an effect similar to calorie restriction, a proven way to extend life. Sirtris hopes they can develop a drug that will effectively combat diseases of aging, including diabetes, Alzheimer's, and cancer.

A weight-reducing, life-extending medicine is about as bold a vision as can exist. "At the beginning, we didn't really have anything to prove it," Christoph told me, when we met at his modest, even drab office nestled in the heart of life sciences innovation, Cambridge, Massachusetts. "We had a little data and a few yeast cells. So, the odds of making it happen were maybe a one percent chance. But, look, there are six billion people on the planet. Everyone is getting older. Nobody wants to die. The science looked real. And, if we're right, if there really are genes we can identify that control the aging process, and we can ultimately get a drug to market, it could be a game changer. I saw this as the kind of opportunity that would be pretty hard to find again."

Actually, it was as much a *story* as it was a vision, a story that Christoph had first glimpsed in 2003. At the time, he was a general partner at Polaris Ventures, a well-regarded venture capital firm in Boston, and had already co-founded five companies, having served as founding CEO at four of them.

In the fall of 2003, he happened upon an article in *Nature* magazine co-authored by Dr. A. David Sinclair, a researcher at MIT, and several colleagues. "In diverse organisms, calorie restriction slows the pace of aging and increases maximum lifespan," Christoph read in that journal. "In the budding yeast *Saccharomyces cerevisiae*, calorie restriction extends lifespan by increasing the activity of Sir2, a member of the conserved sirtuin family. . . ." To the normal person, even to most entrepreneurs, that paragraph may not have jumped out—assuming, that is, they had been reading *Nature* in the first place. To Christoph, son of two doctors and the holder of an MD/PhD from Harvard Medical School (earned in a near-record six years), it made for compelling reading.

Christoph reached out to Dr. Sinclair and went to meet with him. They hit it off. After six months of discussion, they decided to found a business together with the mission of developing a drug out of Dr. Sinclair's research that could help patients live longer, healthier lives. Hundreds of thousands of *Nature*'s readers probably read Dr. Sinclair's article. A true entrepreneur, Christoph was the one who took action.

Christoph left his life as a general partner at a VC firm, took an 80 percent cut in pay, and became founding CEO of Sirtris. "Everyone thought it was a pretty big mistake, including my wife. We had just bought a new house and had a third kid on the way. I had never made much money in venture capital. So, financially, we were exposed." Christoph's VC friends told him he was not behaving rationally. (That sounded very familiar to me.) But, he said, "I was excited about Sirtris in a way I had not been at my other companies."

During the spring and summer of 2004, Christoph and Dr. Sinclair went on a road show, presenting their plan to a number of VC firms. Christoph displayed his boundless optimism, presented his extraordinary vision, both tempered with what proved to be a disarming paranoia. "I'm incredibly paranoid," Christoph confessed to me in one of those genuinely self-effacing ways only extraordinarily successful people can pull off. "I assume that everything is going to go wrong. Paranoia is part of what drives a lot of entrepreneurs in a positive direction, just worrying that everything is going to go wrong and trying to mitigate every possible risk. As Intel's Andrew Grove said, 'Only the paranoid survive.'" The VCs bought the story and appreciated Christoph's candor. He raised $5 million in initial financing, co-led by his former firm Polaris, to kick-start the company and recruit a team to pursue the opportunity.

CONFIDENCE THAT CREATES CONFIDENCE FROM OTHERS

An entrepreneur must be a confident person, of course, but it is not enough to be confident in oneself. The entrepreneur has to inspire confidence in others, which is a wholly different challenge. Much of entrepreneurship is making people feel confident about something in which they really have no basis to believe, because it doesn't exist, and for which there is no proof that it will succeed. To achieve this, entrepreneurs need to demonstrate passionate, authentic leadership, not simple bravado or good salesmanship.[1]

---

1. Bill George of Harvard Business School and former CEO of Medtronic wrote an excellent leadership book, *Authentic Leadership*, that expands on the nature of passionate, mission-driven leaders that lead from the heart, something many great entrepreneurs do with gusto.

Entrepreneurs have to persuade investors to risk capital in a concept that is often little more than a glimmer of an idea. They have to persuade talented professionals to become employees in a company that is not yet a company and has no guarantee of growth or longevity—and often the people the entrepreneur wants most are ones who are already successful and have high-paying jobs and secure positions in well-established companies. Entrepreneurs must also persuade early customers to take a risk on an unproven product or service that may not work, and could even have some unexpected, possibly unwanted, results.

Christoph's Sirtris is a remarkable case study in entrepreneurial power that inspires confidence in others. Even as he was raising capital, Christoph went about instilling enough confidence in others that he was able to build an incredible organization.

He started with what's known as a scientific advisory board, essentially a group of advisers with expert knowledge and world-class networks. An advisory board is a useful mechanism to attract outstanding people with deep domain knowledge to your company. In creating a strong advisory board, an entrepreneur can create a self-fulfilling prophecy, giving the company an aura of success even before it has proved anything. Christoph is a master at this, and other entrepreneurs can follow his lead. In Christoph's case, he wanted a pedigree-rich SAB. It included Nobel Prize–winning biologist Philip Sharp from MIT and gene-cloning researcher Thomas Maniatis, a former senior executive from Merck, as well as MIT professor Robert Langer.

Langer is one of fourteen Institute Professors at MIT, the

highest honor awarded to a faculty member. He holds more than 760 issued or pending patents worldwide (believed to be second only to Thomas Edison, who had 1,093 patents) and has

Bob Langer

licensed or sublicensed many of his patents to some 220 pharmaceutical, chemical, biotechnology, and medical device companies. He has published over one thousand articles and is both the most cited engineer in history and the most prolific inventor in the history of medicine. He has garnered some 180 major awards and, in 1999, was named by *Forbes* magazine as

one of the twenty-five most important individuals in biotechnology in the world. One of my partners likes to refer to Langer as a national treasure, and, in the opinion of many, that is no exaggeration.

Of course, one does not inspire confidence in people like Bob Langer through bluster or bravado. Remember, Christoph had the medical and scientific chops to speak with conviction and in detail to people operating at the highest levels of scientific inquiry and invention. He could also do the talking in French, German, or Spanish, if required.

To me, one of the most striking demonstrations of Christoph's confidence—and his ability to inspire confidence in others—came during the early trials of the drug formulations. There are strict regulations on how and when natural substances like resveratrol can be formulated and tested on humans. Typical practice is to conduct a clinical trial using the services of a partner or subcontractor, many of which are based in India; this requires approval of the Food and Drug Administration (FDA), which can take months or even years.

The senior team at Sirtris decided to test the drugs on themselves, which involved injecting the formulations. "It was in 2004–05 and we were raising our Series B financing," Christoph said. Series B simply means a second round of financing, usually sought after achieving some tangible and positive result following the first round of financing, known as Series A. "We tested six different formulations in me, Peter Elliot, our head of development, David Sinclair, and a few others. So we had track marks on our arms and it's summer and we're in our T-shirts or have our sleeves rolled up. We'd be making a pitch and our arms were all black and blue. The VCs would say, 'What's that?' And we'd say, 'Oh, we're just doing our clinical studies.' They'd think we were a little crazy, but it's okay to be a little crazy. We shaved six months off the development time."

There's a saying that technology companies should eat their own dog food—that is, use their own technology for the purpose it was developed (for example, Microsoft running its internal systems on Microsoft software). But Christoph was taking the concept one step further—he wasn't just eating his own dog food, he was injecting himself with it! It is this kind of confidence and personal commitment, sprinkled in with a dash of what seems like insanity, that builds an almost equal amount of confidence from venture capitalists. VCs like to see entrepreneurs who are committed to their venture. And here was an entrepreneur who had quit his comfortable general partner job at a venture capital firm, recruited some of the top minds in the country to his advisory board, and believed so much in the compound he was developing that he injected himself with it.

Christoph's fund-raising proved to be successful. In March 2005, Sirtris secured $27 million in Series B financing, which would be used to finance further R&D efforts, conduct clinical trials in India, and run lab experiments. Their studies showed that rats that were fed high-calorie diets with resveratrol could run farther, stayed leaner, and lived 30 percent longer than rats that were fed the same diet but without resveratrol.

Sirtris published many of its findings in academic journals or shared them with the popular press. This was a gamble. On the one hand, positive exposure in the academic literature might attract the attention of a potential partner, preferably a large pharmaceutical company that would have the clout to help Sirtris commercialize its drug—which is an expensive, complex, and time-consuming process that requires expertise and resources that Sirtris could not match.

On the other hand, such publicity might simply give away the company's secrets and encourage competitors to develop their own drugs. But Christoph had sufficient confidence that other companies would not be able to capitalize on their findings more successfully, or faster, than Sirtris could. Sure enough, the big pharmaceutical companies took notice. Throughout 2006, Christoph had conversations with several that wanted to form some kind of partnership or make some kind of a deal. "A certain large pharmaceutical learned everything about us and started calling. In fact, they went all the way to the altar with us [i.e., went far down the path in trying to purchase the company], before changing direction and starting their own program. My team got angry. But I said, 'Look, they are a huge company. It'll take them five years to get organized.' "

The exposure in the press and the interest from industry giants further fueled Christoph's confidence, if it needed any more fueling. Soon, it was not even necessary to take the Sirtris show on the road, because so many people came to them. Not long after the *Wall Street Journal* story appeared, Christoph received an email from John Henry, hedge fund mogul and owner of the Boston Red Sox, asking to meet. "After we presented the company, John Henry says, 'How can I be helpful to you?' And I looked at him, and I said, 'I think you could invest fifty million dollars in the company.' And he said, 'I don't think I can do fifty million, but I think I can do twenty million.' And I asked, 'Can we close in two weeks?' "

It took a little longer than that, but not much. In February 2007, Christoph closed on a round of $35.9 million, including contributions from John Henry and Peter Lynch, the legendary Fidelity Investments Magellan fund manager. "Everybody wanted in after that," said Christoph.

Anyone who invests in a biotech firm knows that drug development takes a long time, and payoff can be several years out, if it comes at all—in fact, the majority of new compounds developed by biotech start-ups fail to earn FDA approval. Christoph had sufficient confidence in his idea, his research, and his team to go for the big win. But he was also realistic enough to know that to take the long journey toward uncertain reward might try the patience of even his most committed venture capitalists. So, in 2007, Christoph took Sirtris public.

The IPO enabled his investors to realize a return on their investment (if they chose to sell in the public offering—many didn't), and it raised about $63 million that Sirtris could invest in further research and development.

Then, less than a year later, Christoph and his management team sold their newly public company to its most attractive suitor, GlaxoSmithKline (GSK). GSK had been in conversation with Christoph—just as others had—for several years. In April 2008, GSK acquired Sirtris for $720 million. With GSK's continued support, various drug compounds from Sirtris are in clinical trials for diabetes and diseases of aging, and initial results appear promising.

The acquisition was notable not only for the large amount of money that GSK invested but also because of the confidence the company's leaders felt in Christoph and Sirtris to bring change to the parent company. "When you make an acquisition of a company like Sirtris," said Andrew Witty, CEO of GSK, "you are making a value equation on a belief more than anything else, but hopefully a well-informed belief, based on evidence. The belief is that the platform is going to be a potential fertile ground for a portfolio of products."

In other words, Sirtris was built on Christoph's confidence, sold on his confidence, and brought confidence to those around him—even the leaders of a much older, larger, and more established company than his own. For an entrepreneur, being able to project and inspire confidence is critical.

However, more than confidence is required. Another element that is critical for successful entrepreneurs is an unwavering passion for what they're doing. In the face of obstacles, distractions, and naysayers, great entrepreneurs follow their passion no matter what the odds. The founding of Twitter, an emerging worldwide phenomenon, brings those lessons out in spades.

PURSUING YOUR PASSION: *WHY COURIERS ARE SO COOL*

Jack Dorsey (a.k.a. @jack in the lingo of the Twitterverse) founded Twitter, the social networking and microblogging site where users—Twitterers—post very short (140 characters, tops) updates known as tweets. Twitterers follow other users' tweets and create online communities based on one simple question: "What are you doing?" Although Twitter does

Jack Dorsey

not release company metrics, public data suggest it has over two hundred million users as of early 2011 and is growing rapidly. According to the Web-tracker Hitwise, Twitter traffic jumped 43 percent in one day alone after Oprah Winfrey posted her first on-air tweet on April 17, 2009.

The concept for Twitter came out of Jack's lifelong fascination with mapping the real-time movements of people and things within complex environments. "Since I was very small, I've been fascinated by how cities work," Jack told me in his typically straightforward way. "I always got really excited when I thought about visualizing them, specifically around maps. What would you place on a map to show how a city worked?"

In St. Louis, where he grew up, Jack first noticed the

existence of something he found magical: couriers. "I loved couriers. You had this transfer of physical information happening throughout the city and the world. Someone picking up the package, putting it in a bag, going somewhere, taking it out of the bag, giving it to someone else. I thought that was so cool. I wanted to map it, to see that flow on a big screen. When I did some research into how courier systems worked, I found that there was a parallel information transfer that was digital, and it was called 'dispatch,' which was just a coordination effort."

Jack so loved the idea of digitally mapping interactions around a city and the notion of couriers as a physical manifestation of these interactions that he decided to start a bicycle courier service of his own at the age of sixteen. "I put my brother and me on bikes, just so I could write the dispatch software. [A self-proclaimed computer geek, Jack taught himself to code software at a young age.] We quickly found out that St. Louis had no need for bicycle couriers at all. But I really enjoyed writing the software and getting to the point where I could map and visualize the work."

The rapid demise of his teenage start-up did not deter Jack. While in the second year of an engineering program at the Missouri University of Science and Technology, he came across a New York City–based company called Dispatch Management Services Corporation (DMSC), which managed dispatch centers for couriers—on foot, bicycles, and motorcycles.

"I had to get into that!" Jack enthused, as our conversation took him back in time. "I got in contact with the chairman, Greg Kidd, the guy who had built the company and taken it public. I said, 'I'm writing some dispatch software, and I'd really love to come to New York and work with you all.'" Jack pursued Greg hard, and within a couple of weeks, he moved to New York, transferred to NYU, and started writing dispatch software for DMSC.

At DMSC, Jack delved deeper into his fascination with dispatch and couriers. "There was an essence of communication there," he described to me. "An abstraction. You have all these entities roaming about, and they're all reporting what they're doing in real time over a variety of different devices. We had couriers on CB [citizens band] radios, on PDAs [personal digital assistants], and on cell phones. We had taxis and emergency vehicles with GPS. They're all reporting constantly where they are and what work they're doing, and it's all flowing into this one system that a dispatcher can view in real time on a map. That's what's going on in the city! I thought that abstraction was so cool that I wanted that same thing for my friends."

Jack and Greg decided they could improve on the DMSC dispatch system. In 1998, they moved to the West Coast and raised enough money from the Band of Angels (a group of current and former Silicon Valley executives who provide seed financing to technology entrepreneurs) to found dNET, Dispatch Network. "We wanted to do a Web-centric dispatch system that would essentially provide an ATM for couriers, most of whom don't have bank accounts, so they could easily draw their commissions through the Web."

While he was working to get dNET off the ground, Jack discovered Instant Messaging (IM). "IM is interesting because you look at your buddy list and, at a glance, see what your friends are listening to, what they're working on, what they're doing.

The problem was that you were bound to the computer keyboard. I was fortunate enough to have a RIM 850, the predecessor to the BlackBerry. It was this squat, little email device. One night, I couldn't sleep, I just had to write a prototype script. It would sit on a server, take incoming emails, broadcast them out to a list, and also record them in a database that I could view on the Web." That was the first glimmer of Twitter.

But for a variety of reasons, dNET did not get traction in the market, and so Jack embarked on a period of freelance programming before joining a podcasting start-up called Odeo, primarily to work with Evan (a.k.a. @ev) Williams, formerly of Google. But Jack's brief foray into podcasting didn't squelch his passion for brief status messaging. "At that time, one of my co-workers introduced me to SMS (short message service), which I had never seen before. She used it all the time. Once I saw that, I'm like, 'Whoa, this is awesome!' This communication blew my mind, and the way she was using it blew my mind. I thought, What if we simply set status, archive it on the Web, use SMS to do it, and it all happens in real time? We all kind of went into a corner, wrote out a bunch of user scenarios, and started inviting co-workers in. They fell in love with it. We knew we had something."

Thus, Jack and his team developed the service we now know as Twitter. They called it "Twttr" at the time and launched it in July 2006. The very first tweet was an internal one that Jack sent out at 12:50 P.M. on March 21, 2006: "just setting up my twttr." A few minutes later, he tweeted innocuously: "inviting coworkers." This was the beginning of the Twitter revolution.

Interestingly, Jack pursued a strategy very similar to Christoph's strategy with Sirtris: Don't hide what you're doing and worry about operating stealthily. If you think you're doing something interesting, get it out in the open, shout it out from the rooftops, and solicit as much feedback and input as possible. This strategy was particularly relevant for an Internet-based consumer service like Twitter.

The initial reviews after the launch were mixed. One blogger reacted negatively, calling it "the dumbest thing ever! Who would want all their personal text messages on a public website for anyone to read and track?"[2] Despite such skepticism, the service began to gain momentum and a grassroots following while still hidden inside Odeo. "We knew it was getting big and were just waiting for a trigger. That turned out to be South by Southwest, in 2007."

South by Southwest is a festival and conference—replete with panels, book readings, conversations, and parties—hosted in Austin, Texas, each year. It has three parts: music, film, and interactive. The interactive track focuses on emerging technology and is particularly popular with entrepreneurs and technologists. Jack and his colleagues lugged big plasma screens across the country and set them up in the hallways of the conference to display the live Twitter chatter about the conference sessions in action, one at the registration desk and one at the exit from the main conference room.

"We were really good at getting the right friends in. We had a lot of high-powered, vocal bloggers using Twitter at South by Southwest. They were talking about it non-stop at the conference. And the press happened to be watching, too. And it just blew up."

"Twitter, a simplified blogging service, is hot at South by

---

2. Comment posted on TechCrunch, July 15, 2006: "Odeo Releases Twttr."

Southwest," wrote *InformationWeek* reporter Mitch Wagner in his March 13, 2007, blog post. "Twitter is a service that lets people post one or two short sentences, using phone texting, the Web, email, or chat, and read updates from others through the same channels. You can subscribe to networks of friends or like-minded people; there's a Twitter group set up for South by Southwest. John Edwards, a Democratic presidential candidate, seems to have a Twitter account."

Jack was confident that Twitter would take off, but even he was surprised by the enthusiasm it generated. "This very simple message and subscriber model worked for everything I was interested in. I thought it could be massive. But, as a consumer application, I was really surprised by the velocity and by the patience that our early users had to get it right."

While Twitter was gaining momentum, the start-up that owned the company, Odeo, wasn't. In fact, Odeo had run out of money and didn't have additional funding support from its venture capital investor. Odeo's CEO, Evan Williams, decided to buy the assets from the investors, taking Jack, another co-founder, Biz Stone (@Biz), and many of the employees with him. Jack became Twitter's founding CEO, and thirty days later the team started thinking about raising capital and spinning out as a separate company. "We weren't really ready to take money right away, but we got a note from someone. We went to meet them for breakfast at the top of this hotel in San Francisco and had a pretty good conversation. We were still kind of forming the company and whatnot. When we got back to the office thirty minutes later, we found a scanned image of a check for half a million dollars in our inbox."

The instant offer of funding prompted Jack to think through what he really wanted in an investment partner. "The way the company and the product gained traction was that we got the best people we could think of and we worked with them. And we wanted the same thing from our VC. We wanted the best person across the table from us. It was not where he comes from, but 'Is this guy fun to work with? Is he going to challenge us? Is he smart?' This person was going to take a seat on the board. I viewed it as a hire that we could never fire."

As it turned out, Twitter went with a VC who found the Twitter concept just as fascinating as Jack did. Who was this VC and how did Jack react to him? That's a story for Chapter 4.

The lesson for me as I reflected on the Jack Dorsey story is the power of passion. Jack didn't start Twitter to make money. He had a passion for electronically tracking the activities of his friends and other people. As of 2011, Twitter has raised over $400 million in capital and is valued at over $8 billion. This blindingly simple service has taken the nation by storm. Celebrities from Oprah to Shaquille O'Neal to Senator John McCain are active twitterers. And all because a kid and former bicycle courier from St. Louis wanted an easy way to keep track of his friends, ignoring the doubters who said it wouldn't amount to anything.

CHANGING THE GAME TO CHANGE THE WORLD:
MAKE MONEY SO YOU CAN DO GOOD

When I was a kid, listening at the kitchen table, my parents never talked about money. In my conversations with Christoph

Westphal, Jack Dorsey, and the dozen other entrepreneurs I spoke with for this book, the subject of money was always in the background, of course, but never the most important factor in their deciding to become an entrepreneur. "I think it's very interesting to learn about the human body," Christoph observed. "I've always been fascinated by how cities work," Jack told me.

So, the entrepreneurial drive usually stems from something quite personal and individual.[3] But look a little deeper and you'll find that the really successful entrepreneurs, no matter how large their egos may be, are not usually in the game just to follow their interests. They also want to change the game in their industry and disrupt the status quo. And, more often than not, they want to fundamentally change the world for the better, at least as they interpret what "better" means.

Even those entrepreneurs who are focused on money (and many are) still think of their entrepreneurial journey as a means to make a big impact on the world. King C. Gillette, one of America's earliest and most famous entrepreneurs, didn't particularly care about shaving. He wanted to develop a product with a disposable component—in this case, the blade—that would ensure a continuous stream of revenue. What Gillette really wanted to do was use his money to create a gigantic utopian community—a glass-domed, pollution-free beehive perched at the brink of Niagara Falls and powered

---

3. The individual, personal motivations of an entrepreneur play a huge role in whether they are even comfortable taking VC money in the first place. Harvard Business School Professor Noam Wasserman's research in this area is very illuminating. His course, "Founder's Dilemma," explores what he calls the "Rich versus King" choice, where entrepreneurs must decide whether they care more about money or power when launching and financing their venture. See www.founderresearch.blogspot.com and his *Harvard Business Review* article.

by the flow of its cascade, where sixty million people would live in peace and harmony. Talk about an audacious visionary seeking to change the world.

Reid Hoffman is one of those kinds of entrepreneurs. He is the founder and chairman of the ubiquitous business utility LinkedIn, with one hundred million users, and one of the

Reid Hoffman

most extraordinary and prescient of Silicon Valley's entrepreneurs—and also an angel investor in Facebook, Flickr, Zynga, and many others. Reid is also a "public intellectual" (his own term) and a dozen other things, including a blacksmith and movie maven. For Reid, the driving force behind entrepreneurship is to do good for the world.

Reid had a particular view about how he could and would do some good. Although he is an intellectual with ample credentials (he studied symbolic systems at Stanford and earned a master's of philosophy [MPhil] at Oxford on a Marshall Scholarship), he knew that academia would not be his calling. "Entrepreneurship was my preferred angle of attack," he told me, "because I could impact millions of people that way."

He also believed that academia was out of touch with the way the world was changing. "Today, every individual is a small business," Reid told me. "The idea that you will work for one company for forty years is dead. It's even dead in Japan. It's dead everywhere. Now, you're your own small business charting your own path, and there are entrepreneurial aspects to that. How do you get your next gig? How do you manage the brand of yourself?" As Reid sees it, educators don't understand that the world has changed in this way. "Our educational curriculum has not been updated for a long time," he told me. "If you think about how fast modern life is accelerating, academia is getting more and more out of date."

Knowing he aspired to be an entrepreneur, Reid returned from Oxford to California and took a job at Apple. "To prepare to start your own company, I thought you should go and learn how to ship a software product. Then, you're ready."

In 1997, Reid founded Socialnet, one of the earliest social networking sites, and quickly discovered that he was in over his head. "I realized that I wasn't ready at all," Reid said. "Starting from scratch, building something, a whole company and product, is a very different experience than iterating on something that's already there. The whole entrepreneurial thing is that you kind of jump off a cliff and assemble your airplane on the way down. And financing, by the way, is a thermal draft, right? You're a little further away, but the ground's still coming at you if you can't build an airplane."

While Reid struggled to construct the Socialnet airplane, he kept talking with a close friend, Peter Thiel, who invited Reid to join him in a new venture called PayPal. PayPal's mission was to leverage the Internet as a mechanism to transfer money between consumers. It represented the potential for electronic commerce at its best—helping facilitate payments in a cheaper, more convenient manner. In December 1998, Reid joined the board. "In November 1999, I decided that I was going to leave Socialnet. I helped them hire a new CEO and raise another round of financing, because I thought that was all kind of in the honor category, and then I was going to go start another company. And when I told Peter that, he said, 'No, no, no. Don't do that. Join us here at PayPal.' And so, in January 2000, I joined the company full-time."

The plan was to sell PayPal within six months, but it ended up taking three years. During that time, Reid began to realize that in order to have the freedom to make a major impact in the world, he needed some real money. "I needed a 'ransom' that would let me say, 'Now I can choose how I want to spend my time, with no impediments.' I needed not to have to earn a salary." In 2002, eBay acquired PayPal for $1.5 billion and Reid had his ransom. "Because of PayPal, I could live comfortably for the rest of my life, take care of my kids and everything else. So I was, like, 'Okay, now what do I care about?' Well, ultimately what I care about is making a big, scalable impact on the world. And I realized, 'All right, I don't have enough money to create big, new non-profit institutions. I only have enough money for me. So why don't I go and do a really good thing on the for-profit side?'"

That was LinkedIn. Reid felt he could make an impact by helping people easily connect with friends and colleagues to improve their lives and professional activities. "LinkedIn had something to do with how I think the Internet works, how it changes people's lives."

In order to raise money, Reid had to provide more than just a "change the world" mantra, but also a business pitch. In his early discussions with VCs in early 2003, they pressed him for more specifics. "Investors said, 'Okay, great, we see that big vision, but what's the specific thing?'" Reid recalls. "And I said, 'The specific thing starts as a way of connecting with other professionals, establishing a profile, and communicating with them.' But you need to be a lot more specific in order to raise money. So, I just said, 'Forget it, I'll finance it myself. I'll get the first specific thing up. And then I'll use that as a basis for financing and everything else.'" Starting small, Reid felt he could build momentum without spending a lot of money, simply by building a great product that had real utility. It's a lesson I like to cite for aspiring entrepreneurs who want to raise money before they've proven anything out. It is always more impressive to investors when you are so confident in your idea and your ability to build it that you just go ahead and do it on a shoestring budget and have something tangible to show investors.

Reid was right to be confident in his abilities and the intrinsic value of the service he was building. He launched a beta version of the service in May 2003 and began to see initial traction as he and his founding team invited their own personal networks to join the community. LinkedIn grew rapidly and virally, doubling in size every six weeks, as members joined and then invited their professional colleagues to "link" with them. The company did eventually attract VC money and grew in value. In its first round of financing, led by Sequoia Capital in October 2003, the company raised under $5 million. Since then the company has raised over $100 million in private capital and had a very successful IPO in June 2011, resulting in a $9 billion market valuation. The company has been profitable since 2006 and is an important part of the connective tissues for businesspeople around the world.

But for Reid, it has never been about stacking up money or showing it off. Until the summer of 2008, Reid and his wife lived in a small two-bedroom apartment. He prefers books to clothes. "Money is nice, right?" he confessed to me. "Money gives you good things, it gives you a power that you can go do other things with. But it's not a meaning of a life in itself. Money is a motivator, but it's not the motivator that I wake up in the morning thinking about, it's not the motivator that I go home thinking about, it's not the motivator that gets you an obituary. It's the enabler of a large variety of other things. LinkedIn can have a big positive impact in itself and will also generate money that I could use to do other things. Things that enable you to say, 'Yes, the world is a better place because I was here.'"

That's how the great entrepreneurs think. The money is nice and appreciated, but, as mentioned before, it's almost never about the money. It's about passion, following a dream, and changing the world (with plenty of craziness along the way). And to help them along with advice and capital, many entrepreneurs turn to the venture capitalist.

2

INSIDE THE VC CLUB:
THE ONE THOUSAND DECIDERS

No kid dreams of growing up to become a venture capitalist.

I certainly didn't when I was a student, and that's still true of students today. When they are asked what they want to be when they graduate from college, a large percentage of students reply, "Entrepreneur." To have a dream and build it into a success is indeed fundamental to the American system of capitalist free enterprise. Some of our greatest cultural icons— from Thomas Edison to Steve Jobs—have been entrepreneurs.

Few, if any, students mention the goal of becoming a venture capitalist. Although the VC industry has gained prominence since my college days, most students I've talked to still don't know what a venture capitalist is or how a VC firm operates. There are no Thomas Edisons among the VC ranks. Even John Doerr—legendary for helping to launch Netscape, Google, and Amazon.com—is hardly a household name.

So it's not surprising that kids don't see the glory in a life dedicated to enabling others to become heroes. What budding entrepreneur would volunteer to play Robin instead of Batman?

But although the majority of entrepreneurs have no interest in themselves becoming VCs, it is critical that they understand their backgrounds and motivations to better understand what makes them tick.

As those of us who have been fortunate enough to stumble upon the world of venture capital have discovered, being a VC is a great gig.

THE ALLURE OF THE OTHER SIDE

After ten years as an entrepreneur working for three start-ups, I had learned a lot about fledgling companies. I had also come to understand the critical role of the venture capitalists. Ever so gradually, I began to wonder how life might look if I went over to the mysterious "other side." Still, when two VC friends (Michael Greeley, formerly of Polaris Ventures, and Chip Hazard, formerly of Greylock) called and said, "Jeff, we've started a VC firm. Do you want to join us?" I surprised myself at how quickly I said yes. In hindsight, I think I was ready for a new challenge and eager to approach the VC business as an entrepreneur.

When I hung up my entrepreneurial spikes, my start-up friends had a range of reactions. "You've gone over to the Dark Side!" some of them teased. Others saw VCs quite differently, as all-powerful "Masters of the Universe." As I soon learned, neither of these extreme perspectives was an accurate reflection of the essence of the venture capitalist.

Just as I was fortunate to learn from great mentors during my tenure as an entrepreneur, I've learned a great deal from my VC partners and their collective experience. The firm we have built, Flybridge Capital Partners, now has over half a billion dollars under management across three funds and, at the time of this writing, has made investments in roughly fifty portfolio companies in which it owns a share (typically 15–25 percent). The five general partners (shortly after we started, the three of us were joined by David Aronoff of Greylock and entrepreneur Jon Karlen) focus on the very earliest stage of the venture capital spectrum—the first money in, typically not long after a company's inception.

I have found that being a VC entails a very different kind of excitement than entrepreneurship does. It offers intellectual adventure, exposure to amazing people with brilliant new ideas, and the chance to make a positive impact on the world. I have found far fewer ups and downs as a VC as compared to being an entrepreneur. As an entrepreneur, the emotional roller-coaster ride is such that the highs are very high ("We're going to rule the world!") and the lows are very low ("We're going to miss payroll and go out of business!"). For the VC, there's a greater emotional detachment—to which it has taken time for me to adjust. I don't get to personally create products or companies or lead teams. The VC is the backer of a movie in which he never stars, but he prefers it that way. As a VC he would rather be the enabler and facilitator than the builder or onstage performer. The best VCs are people who tend to get bored working on one business at a time in an in-depth fashion. They are notorious BlackBerry addicts and, because of their hyperactive minds and love for rapid, varied stimulation, have the attention span of someone suffering from attention deficit disorder.

WELCOME TO THE VC CLUB

The VC club is small and exclusive. There are a limited number of routes that lead to its door. Like me, other VCs have found themselves stepping over the VC threshold as the result of some chance encounter. There is no degree that prepares someone to become a VC, but the venture capitalists I know seem to have some common characteristics. They are intelligent, fantastically curious, omnivorous, driven to success, competitive, and often a bit geeky.

Perhaps it's no wonder then that the entire worldwide venture capital industry—if you can call it an industry—consists of fewer than six thousand people working in less than a thousand firms. The National Venture Capital Association (NVCA) estimates that there were 790 venture capital firms in existence in 2010 in the United States. This means that 790 firms had raised money to make investments within the previous eight years; it does not mean that all of them were actually making new investments in 2010. In fact, they estimate that a substantially smaller number, perhaps four hundred, are active in funding start-ups at the time of this writing. Of the six thousand investment professionals working in these firms, only a thousand of them can be classified as major players who make investment decisions and sit on the boards of directors. To reiterate—the decisions that lead to the funding for and aiding of the companies that account for over 20 percent of the gross domestic product of the United States and, in addition, provide medical care for one in three Americans are made by only about one thousand individuals.

One of the common factors that ties members of the VC club to each other is that a large number of them emerge from the same schools: among the most popular are the college and business schools of Harvard and Stanford universities. A handful of other Ivy League schools and MIT are also frequent common denominators. Over 95 percent of the major players are men.[4] Because VCs often invest in groups (often two or three firms will invest together in a particular start-up), there are frequent overlapping relationships from being co-investors and board members together in various start-ups.

The venture capital industry is also highly concentrated geographically. Silicon Valley is the epicenter of the VC world and of everyone who aspires to enter it. My hometown of Boston, Massachusetts, is a strong number two, in large part because Harvard and MIT serve as a training ground for great entrepreneurial and technical talent, and VCs follow the talent. The statistics suggest that the capital is concentrated. According to the NVCA, approximately $80 billion of the $180 billion of total VC capital under management resides in

---

4. The preponderance of males in VC is a stubborn phenomenon. Some researchers, such as Professor Myra Hart of Harvard Business School, believe it will change as more women enter feeder fields such as engineering and biotechnology. The industry's tightly woven, clubby nature is a factor as well. "Women trying to launch or further careers as VCs have fewer first-degree connections with those [men] in positions to hire or promote them." (Kauffman Institute study, "Gateways of Venture Growth.")

California. Thirty billion dollars is managed in Massachusetts and $17 billion in New York. Those three states alone represent 70 percent of all capital under VC management. Thus, imagine the fewer than one thousand senior VCs spending their time shuttling back and forth between Silicon Valley, Boston, and New York City, all tightly interconnected through their college and business school alumni networks, interlocking business and personal relationships, and all connected by no more than one degree of separation using social networking tools like Reid Hoffman's LinkedIn, Jack Dorsey's Twitter, or Mark Zuckerberg's Facebook. There are exceptions to every rule and this description is obviously a general characterization, but in short, that is the general essence of the astoundingly tightly woven VC club.

As a member of this club, I am pleased to take you inside for a tour—with the help of several of its most successful and long-standing members. We'll look at the different kinds of VC firms, consider the process they follow in identifying and choosing deals, see how they make their money, and plumb their psyches to see what motivates them. Many VCs are open and transparent once you get access to them. And as you'll see from the examples below, many of them are creative in their use of social media to improve transparency and accessibility.

NO ONE ELSE DOES EXACTLY WHAT THE VC DOES

Before we open the door, I want to put the VC club into a broader context, because the venture-backed start-up is a very specific kind of funding opportunity. Most other sources of capital or funding available to business enterprises are not interested in, willing to, or able to get involved in high-risk ventures that have uncertain outcomes and long payouts.

The vast majority of the six hundred thousand companies that are started every year in the United States do not receive funding from venture capital. What other routes do entrepreneurs take to raise money for their new businesses? Some entrepreneurs have the wherewithal to reach into their pockets and put up their own start-up money. In some cases, this could be tens of thousands of dollars from savings or credit cards. In other cases, the start-up capital required to bootstrap a business could be hundreds of thousands or even millions of dollars that might have come from a "liquidity event"—such as selling a previous company or receiving a large payout from a stock holding or golden parachute. But very, *very* few entrepreneurs have the kind of capital—usually many millions of dollars—needed to start and build a breakthrough technology venture over five to ten years. They are much more likely to start something that has a reasonably clear path to success and can generate income within a year or two (particularly rare for start-ups involving sophisticated technology with a long development cycle). Or they may tinker with their idea, hire an employee or two, and dribble in money as needed, working out of their basement or garage or in a corner of somebody else's office. Entrepreneurs often also raise money from family and friends but, again, the amounts available and the risk tolerances are relatively low.

Some large companies, especially technology companies like Microsoft, IBM, and Siemens, can also be seen as a type of VC, because they invest funds in what might be thought of as start-up technology ventures within their organizations. They extol the virtues of entrepreneurship, work to instill the spirit of individual enterprise within their employees, and would dearly love to create breakthrough products in their own research and development (R&D) labs—and sometimes do. However, the structure and nature of such ventures are wholly different from those of the venture-capital-backed start-up. This is because genuine entrepreneurs find corporate hierarchies too stifling, and large companies are not likely to fund new initiatives that will cannibalize products in their portfolio, enter entirely unknown markets, or put their own existence in jeopardy. This form of internal entrepreneurship, sometimes called "intrapreneurship," requires too much rule-breaking and cultural transformation to be consistently viable for most large corporations.

That's largely why big companies buy small start-ups: to get the innovation they find difficult to generate from within—the very reason why GSK bought Christoph Westphal's company, Sirtris, or why Dell bought Zing Systems, a Flybridge portfolio company. That type of acquisition is not always successful, of course, because big companies can crush the entrepreneurial spirit of the acquired team rather than be stimulated by it. Christoph acknowledges that his role as a unit leader within GSK is much different from what it was as a co-founder of a start-up. "Prior to the acquisition," he said, "Sirtris was a highly productive, fully integrated place that got things done very quickly. We believe that to continue in this vein, we will need to control everything from discovery through filing of regulatory demands and running early trials. We will need to bring the amazing resources of GSK to bear on Sirtris, but the way we'll keep the entrepreneurial spirit alive is by being pretty self-contained." It will take time to see whether Sirtris's entrepreneurial initiatives can continue inside a major company.

And then there are angel investors. These are individuals, or groups of individuals, who have cash, and usually expertise, to invest. Many angels are themselves former entrepreneurs who can help young entrepreneurs avoid common pitfalls while providing less structure than a VC firm. Usually, they invest without a formal timetable, sometimes in exchange for a smaller ownership stake, and typically without a seat on the board. Many entrepreneurs gravitate to angel investors when they require less capital than a typical VC might be interested in investing (say, less than $2 million), and when they have preexisting relationships with angel investors such that they don't need to go through a long due diligence process. Many angel investors are motivated by economic returns, but many are simply motivated by the thrill of being involved in early-stage start-ups.

In recent years, there has been a surge of angel investing. Over 57,000 entreprenurial ventures received angel investments, with a total of nearly $18 billion invested from 260,000 individuals in 2009.[5] In comparison, only 32,000 companies received angel investments in 2002. Some active angels have formed groups, become professionalized, and behave, in effect, like venture capitalists in terms of their thinking and rigor of analysis. Often the angel investors are seen as helping young start-ups bridge the gap between the raw idea and getting to a point of maturity and momentum, when they can attract venture capital investment.

As they gain more experience and confidence, some angel

---

5. Jeffrey Sohl, "The Angel Investor Market in 2008: A Down Year in Investment Dollars but Not in Deals," Center for Venture Research, March 26, 2009.

investors have become more professional in their approach. In many cases, individual angels join together to form a group to evaluate and invest in new companies, operating much like a VC firm. Some of these angel groups hire professional staff and bump up against VCs in competing for investment opportunities. Many of these groups, known as "super angels" or "micro-VCs," operate regionally (such as the Show Me Angels out of Missouri), and a few have national reputations and practices (such as Ron Conway, a former entrepreneur in Silicon Valley who has made more than five hundred angel investments). Some angel groups are less concerned about making money than they are about helping entrepreneurs and contributing to the start-up ecosystem. Others operate much more like VCs and manage other people's money as well as their own.

LinkedIn's Reid Hoffman is, among his other roles, an active angel investor. He described to me the different types of angels he sees running around Silicon Valley: "There are people [with less domain expertise] who put in a lot of time and energy. They can provide broad support, like helping to recruit people or sorting out things like office leases and that kind of stuff. Then there are people like me, who are very professional and involved in the space, but also extremely busy with a day job and two boards and everything else but can lend their Rolodex to be helpful. Then there are hobbyists, usually retired, who are pretty passive. I generally find that it's better to get one of the first two types."

A venture capital firm offers something that other funding sources generally do not: active participation in the development and management of the start-up business. Typically, at least one partner in the VC firm will take a seat on the board of the company in which it invests. The VC partner often has some knowledge of the particular industry or business area of the start-up, as well as extensive experience in starting and growing a variety of businesses.

So it is a very particular kind of entrepreneurial enterprise that venture capitalists generally fund. Usually it requires an idea with breakthrough, game-changing potential that needs large amounts of capital to get off the ground, typically technology based in some way and a situation that requires high-priced talent (where "price" may mean rich stock packages as much as, or more than, cash compensation). The typical start-up that is a good fit for VC money may not generate any revenue for two to four years, if ever. And the typical entrepreneur who is a good fit for VC money wants and needs the very active participation of the capital provider in the oversight of the business.

THE PLAYERS

A VC firm tends to be organized (often unwittingly) around the thesis of James Surowiecki's book *The Wisdom of Crowds*— that is, no one person can be as smart as a group of informed, independent-minded people. And the way to make the best investment decisions is to construct a democratic process rather than a hierarchical one. Thus, VC firms typically gather a group of experienced investment professionals with diverse backgrounds and perspectives and do not allow any one individual's power or status to sway the discussion. Robust group discussions and debates will ultimately yield better investment decisions than any one, smart individual might alone achieve.

Walking into a VC firm can feel a bit like entering the Clone Wars: everyone looks the same—early thirties to late forties in age, well groomed, sporting khakis and blue button-down shirts. When in a more formal situation, everyone will also have the requisite blue blazer. It's hard to figure out exactly who is who. Unlike most corporate environments, there's often no obvious power relationship between the professionals around the conference table, as VC firms typically collect smart people with strong opinions and then let them rip, regardless of seniority or stature.

Given that essential characteristic, firms organize themselves in different ways. Some are built like classic consulting firms with a pyramid structure where large staffs of more junior professionals surround and support a smaller number of senior partners. For example, Boston-based Bain Capital Ventures (a division of private equity firm Bain Capital) has thirty investment professionals, of whom eight are general partners and the others are either associates, principals, or venture partners working their way up the food chain. Similarly, Battery Ventures has thirty investment professionals, of whom twelve are general partners and the rest are associates, principals, or venture partners. At the other end of the spectrum, Silicon Valley–based Redpoint Ventures has twelve general partners (they call them "partners") as well, but only four non-partner investment professionals. At Flybridge Capital Partners, we have five general partners and only two non-partner investment professionals—more like an inverted pyramid.

Regardless how the firm looks, there are very precise and distinct roles in the VC world: general partners, principals, associates, entrepreneurs in residence, and limited partners.

VC Firm Structure: General Partners (GPs), Principals, and Associates

General partners (sometimes called managing directors or, simply, partners) are the most senior investment professionals in the firm. They decide which start-ups to invest in and sit on the boards of the companies once they're funded. They are often the owners of the firm, although a managing general partner title may be used to distinguish between the general partners who truly manage the firm from those who simply lead certain investments.

Some firms are federations of general partners who operate quite independently, as if they were operating different practices in a law firm or medical practice. In other firms, the general partners work closely together and make their investment decisions collaboratively.

General partners typically have ten to twenty years of experience as a VC, as an entrepreneur, or as an operating executive at a larger company or perhaps even a combination of the two. Many have an MBA or advanced technical degree in relevant fields, such as computer science, electrical engineering, or biochemistry. Many VCs carry their competitive, overachieving nature into their personal interests, for example, becoming accomplished musicians or athletes. (Although I must confess that I have zero musical talent and am a rather mediocre but dedicated weekend warrior.)

Principals are general-partners-in-training and, as a result, very eager to prove themselves to be worthy of promotion. They usually support the general partners in seeking out investment opportunities and in conducting the due diligence needed for them to make investment decisions. They provide input into investment decisions and, in some cases, may have authority to recommend investment opportunities subject to approval by the general partners. Principals usually have three to six years of work experience post-MBA or other graduate school and are younger versions of the general partners—type A, competitive, etc.

Associates support the general partners and principals and have no authority to make investment decisions themselves. Some of them have recently graduated from a top MBA program, most typically from Harvard, Stanford, or Wharton. Others have only an undergraduate degree, usually technical, and are two to four years out of college. Associates will often have worked for a few years in a start-up, a large technology company, or perhaps gotten some business training through a brief stint at a management consulting firm or an investment bank.

For all levels of investment professionals, the more years of experience they have the better. "The venture capital business is fundamentally an apprenticeship business," noted Terry McGuire, co-founder and general partner of Boston-based Polaris Venture Partners and recent chairman of the National Venture Capital Association (NVCA). "There's no school for

Fred Wilson

it. Every truly successful venture capitalist has been mentored in turn by another successful venture capitalist over a long period of time."

Fred Wilson of New York–based Union Square Ventures concurs. With some humility he admitted to me, "It took me a while to really get going in the venture business. I think for my first ten years, I didn't know what I was doing." Fred is an MIT graduate, received his MBA from the Wharton School of Business, and jumped into the VC world shortly after graduation. His investment track record is extraordinary; he was the lead investor in Jack Dorsey's Twitter. If someone as smart and capable as Fred took ten years to figure it out, imagine how long it takes mere mortals.[6]

There are typically two career tracks for VCs: former entrepreneurs or apprenticeship-track professionals who may have been investment bankers or consultants before becoming VCs. There is often debate among entrepreneurs and industry observers over which of the two types of VCs make better venture capitalists. On the one hand, the former entrepreneurs can empathize with the management team and also bring some useful operating skills to the table. On the other hand, professional VCs know their boundaries (i.e., don't interfere with management's purview) and tend to have broader networks and more sophisticated experience with various financing strategies and acquisitions.

On this debate, Fred reflects, "I have never been an entrepreneur and I think that's a bit of a liability that I've overcome just because I've been doing this business for a long time now. But I think that the VCs who have been entrepreneurs, if they can truly make the switch to being a VC, are the best VCs."

Truly making the switch, fully and completely, from entrepreneur to VC is tricky. When I was starting off on my own journey of conversion, Ted Dintersmith of Charles River Ventures warned me, "Remember, you don't run these companies; you invest in great people to run these companies. If you think

---

6. Fred is also a prolific and popular VC blogger. You can find his blog at www.avc.com.

they work for you like divisional presidents, you have it all wrong. In truth, you want to invest in people who are better than you, and make sure you work for them. The entrepreneur is your boss and customer combined." I've never forgotten this sage advice.

Entrepreneurs in Residence (EIR)

There is another player who shows up from time to time in a venture capital firm, the entrepreneur in residence, or EIR. The EIR is generally a former start-up CEO or a would-be CEO who has a special relationship with the VC firm. The EIR may be hired by the VC firm for a six- to twelve-month period with the express purpose of starting up a new company (which the VC firm will be backing) or joining a fledgling start-up as one of the senior executives to help it get rolling and catalyze the firm's investment. When entrepreneurs meet EIRs, they sometimes worry that the EIR is going to steal their idea with the help of the sponsoring VC firm. This has happened on only rare occasions, but the prudent entrepreneur nonetheless should be careful about the downside of divulging too much about their business to an EIR. On the other hand, EIRs can be great entry points into the VC firm if they become enthusiastic sponsors of your idea.

Nitzan Shaer, who had been an executive with eBay and Skype, joined Flybridge as an EIR in 2007. "The idea of becoming an EIR was introduced to me after I started considering my next steps at Skype," Nitzan wrote on my blog, Seeing Both Sides.[7] "I had three options on the table: join an early-stage start-up, start

---

7. www.seeingbothsides.com.

a company of my own, or become an EIR. Honestly, there was no start-up I found that excited me, but there were a bunch of ideas that I wanted to pursue—not all of them in my direct area of expertise, so I knew I would need time and advice."

Nitzan met with eight venture capital firms and discovered that there were "nine different definitions to the term EIR. Boiling it down, there are three areas EIRs typically focus on: identifying new investment opportunities, helping portfolio companies, and ultimately launching or joining a new investment (the 'exit' event for an EIR)."

To succeed as an EIR in the eyes of the VC firm, Nitzan discovered there is just one metric that counts: "Bring at least one investment into the firm that they would not have made otherwise!" While with us, Nitzan identified and helped us assess two investment opportunities, one of which was Transpera, a San Francisco–based mobile video start-up in which we invested and whose board I joined.

The Limited Partner

One very important figure whom you won't actually meet in the office of the VC, but whose presence looms above all proceedings, is the limited partner, or LP. The LP is so important because he, she, or it is the source of the VC's money. Every three to four years, when the venture capital firm is raising a new fund, the partners dash around the country (and sometimes the world) catching up with their LPs, presenting the performance of their portfolio, updating them on any strategy or personnel changes, and then asking again to invest their money in this risky asset class.

There are numerous types of limited partners, including:

Endowments, e.g., universities such as Harvard, Yale, or Stanford

Public Pension Funds, e.g., state pension funds, such as the California pension fund, CALPERS

Corporate Pension Funds, e.g., IBM's pension fund

Sovereign Wealth Funds, e.g., the government of Singapore's investment arm

Wealthy Families, e.g., the Rockefeller family's investment fund

Funds of Funds, e.g., special-purpose funds that are created to provide smaller institutions and families the scale to get into top-tier firms—such as Knightsbridge Advisers and FLAG Ventures

David Swensen, the well-regarded head of the Yale endowment and author of *Unconventional Success: A Fundamental Approach to Personal Investment*, is famous for pointing out that VC returns are highly dependent on which individual firm you invest in. In other words, an LP who is able to invest in one of the top VCs will make much more money, on a relative scale, than in almost any other asset class. But if an LP gets stuck investing in a mediocre VC, they will do very poorly—more poorly than investing in a typically bad mutual fund manager. High risk, high reward. And only a few VCs and LPs seem to get the formula consistently right.

An important subtlety for entrepreneurs to understand is that because VCs have investors in the form of LPs, there is an inherent conflict in their role as board members of your venture. The VC has two loyalties that may occasionally conflict: a fiduciary duty to generate the maximum return for their LPs, and a fiduciary duty to protect the interests of all shareholders in the companies they're investors in, and for which they serve on the boards. When these interests diverge, tension emerges between the VC and the management team that can lead to conflict and drama, which I'll cover later, in Chapter 5.

DIFFERENT FIRMS HAVE DIFFERENT PROFILES

Although most VC firms are structured similarly, they are far from alike. The number of investment opportunities any VC receives is extremely large. For example, at Flybridge, we typically are approached or learn about approximately two thousand businesses seeking capital each year. In addition, the range of industries is incredibly broad (we might get a plan for a new medical device, a piece of software, and an online service in any one day). Therefore, most venture capital firms organize their efforts in some particular way—by becoming generalists or specialists, going global or staying local, investing at a particular stage of a new company's growth.

As with any business, a VC firm needs to make some fundamental business choices that define its particular focus and how it constructs a portfolio of investments over time that matches its strategy. An entrepreneur seeking capital should know and understand these choices to help sort out which kind of VC will most likely invest in what the entrepreneur has to offer, and with which VC they would most likely want to work.

VC Profiles: David Hornik Just Wants to Have Techno Fun

Venture capital firms invest in all kinds of businesses in a wide range of industry sectors, but they have a clear preference for certain kinds of ventures. Consistently, the favored industries for

David Hornik

VC dollars are software (18 percent of total VC investment in the United States in 2009), biotechnology (20 percent), energy/industrial companies (13 percent), and medical devices and equipment (14 percent). VCs don't typically show as much interest in services, either health care or financial, or consumer products and services. While there is always an exception, it tends to be harder to scale these businesses fast enough to drive the kinds of returns that VCs like to see.

David Hornik, forty-two, is a general partner at August Capital, based in Menlo Park, California, where he focuses on information technology companies. One of August Capital's claims to fame is that its founder, David Marquardt, was the first and only institutional investor in Microsoft and still sits on its board of directors. When he launched www .ventureblog.com in 2004, David Hornik was the first venture capitalist to become a blogger (and inspired many others to blog, myself included). He became so enraptured with blogging that he invested in Six Apart, the blogging company that created TypePad and Moveable Type.

David's path to the door of the VC club was perhaps a little more circuitous than most, although it passed through the typical institutions (Harvard and Stanford) and geographies (Boston and Silicon Valley). "I didn't have a master plan that someday I would be a venture capitalist and so, what are the steps I must take to get there," David told me with his signature impish smirk. "In every instance, it was, 'There's an opportunity here that seems interesting and fun.' I jumped at each one. They were all driven by my desire to do fun, interesting things and not worry about the rules too much."

Brought up in Sudbury, Massachusetts, David's polymathic tendencies were encouraged by his father, a computer scientist and one of the early members of the DEC team. In high school, David became particularly interested in synthesized music, leading to an interest in the intersection of computers and music. He chose to go to Stanford, largely because of its Center for Computer Research in Music and Acoustics. I commented to David that many venture capitalists who, like him, are interested in consumer Web initiatives are music enthusiasts. "Yeah, music and creativity and the arts," he replied. "It's an illness, I think. We all try to express some creativity because, as a general matter, the job of the VC involves creativity only by proxy."

At Stanford, David made friends with two seemingly opposing types of characters. He rubbed shoulders with students who later became venture capitalists, such as Steve Jurvetson, now a general partner at Draper Fisher Jurvetson (DFJ). "Steve was the computer coordinator in our dorm," David said, "the guy who was in charge of fixing the computers when they were broken—basically the resident nerd."

There were also would-be entrepreneurs roaming David's Stanford dorm, including Jerry Yang, one of the founders of

Yahoo! David was very fortunate—the Internet revolution would explode in Silicon Valley five years later, and so anyone hanging around Stanford at that time met many of the future leaders of the revolution.

After graduating from Stanford in 1990, David jumped at an opportunity that one might not expect a computer music lover to embrace. He went to the University of Cambridge in England and earned an MPhil in criminology. "I was considering becoming a criminal defense attorney at the time," he told me. This interest in turn led him to attend Harvard Law School, where he earned his JD, and eventually landed at Cravath, Swaine & Moore—one of the celebrated white shoe law firms in New York—as a litigator.

During the time he was there, David was regularly in touch with his old Stanford roommate, who had found his way into the Venture Law Group, which provided counsel to a number of Internet start-ups, including Yahoo! "He was always flying to Japan to negotiate licensing agreements and financing them. And I said, 'Wow, what you're doing sounds a lot more fun than what I'm doing. Why not ask the partners at your firm if they'd be interested in teaching me what you guys do?'"

At Venture Law Group and then another small law firm, David's practice focused primarily on Internet start-ups. He would often participate in his clients' board meetings, attended by both the entrepreneur and the venture capitalists, but he did not behave in a typical lawyerly fashion. "I didn't realize, or chose to ignore the fact," David confessed with a chuckle, "that the appropriate role for the attorney is to stay in the background, take notes, point out instances where the company may be pushing up against thorny legal issues, and be available to answer questions. To my mind, board meetings should be collections of smart people trying to figure out the best path for a company, and I had spent hours and hours working with clients around licensing deals and financings, and I felt like I knew their businesses quite well, so I would share my opinions."

One of the companies David represented was Evite, whose lead investor was August Capital, founded by David Marquardt. Over time, Marquardt began to appreciate David's broader skills beyond legal advice and, after one board meeting, approached David in the parking lot. "Dave Marquardt said to me, 'Have you ever thought about the venture business?'" David Hornik recalled. "To which my answer was, 'I'd love to think about the venture business.' That started the process. Over a four-month period, the partners got comfortable with the idea that—despite the fact that I was a lawyer—I might actually have some hope as a venture investor. I ended up joining the firm in June of 2000."

David ended up in the right place. "August is about as geeky a partnership as you're going to find," David said. "Five of the six partners are engineers." The August Capital partners leverage their expertise in and passion for technology and invest almost solely in early-stage high-tech companies. Their goal is to help their companies grow and create as much value as possible. In that quest, they have kept their fund sizes relatively small, which is typical of specialist or focused venture capital firms. Its most recent fund, closed in March 2009, was $400 million, or roughly $60 million per partner. "We just think that's the right way to do business," David explained. "I'm sure there are plenty of firms out there that are making money from amassing huge funds, and lots of management fees, but we're much more interested in creating big companies that have value. This business is very people-driven and doesn't scale."

David recognizes that having the chance to fund companies that could eventually change the world is a very special place to be. "It's wildly intellectually stimulating," he said. "You're learning something new every day, there are always new challenges. It's just an amazing thing to think that the partners at August Capital were the earliest investors in Microsoft, Seagate, Sun, Compaq, Intuit, and Symantec, companies that have built really interesting products that have changed the way that we live our lives."

Geographical Reach: Going Global or Staying Local

Some VC firms invest only in companies that are a quick drive or an easy plane ride away. The proximity enables them to maintain the old-fashioned culture of a small, focused team of professionals sitting around the table every Monday morning to talk about deals. Other firms seek to build a brand, team, and investment process that can be exported to other geographies around the world.

At Flybridge Capital, we have chosen the local strategy. Like David Hornik, we aren't convinced that venture capital, when practiced at the very early stages, can scale across geographies and industry sectors. Unlike most industries, where there are benefits to consolidation (cost savings, brand power, operational and distribution efficiencies), there are no such economies of scale in the venture business. In fact, some argue there are diseconomies of scale and that the business is still very much an art more than a science, which depends on the judgment of gifted individual investors who see value where others do not. Decisions at larger firms can get delegated to more junior investment professionals and not as much cross-partnership scrutiny is given to each decision.

Some entrepreneurs view geographical dispersion as a negative as compared to geographical focus. When VCs are not physically located close to you, they are less likely to be as helpful or in touch with the ups and downs of your start-up. That is why Silicon Valley–based VCs typically fund Silicon Valley–based firms and Boston-based VCs typically fund East Coast start-ups. There are plenty of exceptions (e.g., Jack Dorsey's Twitter chose Fred Wilson, a New York City–based VC, to be his lead investor), but being close by for a quick chat about strategy, recruiting, product positioning, and financing is beneficial to a productive VC-entrepreneur relationship.

Tim Draper

Entrepreneurs can easily research whether firms make investments out of their office geographies or only make local investments by examining the geographic location of a firm's portfolio companies. Draper Fisher Jurvetson, for example, is the quintessential global venture capital firm. "Want to change the world?" is the bold headline on their home page.

Tim Draper, founder of DFJ and its managing director, was literally born to be a VC—he is the son and grandson of venture capitalists. His grandfather was General William Draper,

Jr., who became the first professional West Coast venture capitalist after serving in the Truman administration as an implementer of the Marshall Plan. His father, Bill Draper, is one of Silicon Valley's legendary venture capitalists and still invests out of his own firm. Tim has created a legacy of his own by investing in early-stage companies, including Skype, Hotmail, and Baidu, the Chinese-based search company that is profiled later in Chapter 7.

DFJ is based in Menlo Park, California, but starting in 2005 began to aggressively expand outside of the United States, with affiliated funds in Israel, Europe, India, China, Vietnam, and others. The model DFJ has taken is analogous to the McDonald's franchise model. Find a local management team, provide them with a brand and back-office support (accounting, fund management, and the like), and create a global network of venture capitalists that are tied together by economic and social bonds, share deals and analysis, yet make investment decisions and control the bulk of their own economics locally.

Sitting down together over cocktails during an industry conference in New York City, I asked Tim—why the drive to expand globally? "I love entrepreneurs," he explained. "I want to find them everywhere. I knew they wouldn't all be in Silicon Valley. Microsoft was in Redmond, Washington; it didn't come from the Silicon Valley or Route 128 outside of Boston. I thought, Where else are deals going to come from? It was a huge step to go international. People looked at me as if I were out of my mind. I partly am. But it worked out really well. I've been to sixty-five different countries and probably funded businesses in thirty of them. It was sort of a risk. But it's made my life much more interesting."

Through this strategy, Tim and DFJ gain a bigger playing field and greater access to more entrepreneurs, which benefit their entrepreneurs, wherever they are. "I think entrepreneurs have better odds with us now, because we try to do something for them," Tim observed. "Maybe a referral to a business that might fund them or to a network partner who's in New York or Chicago or Bangalore. Our hit rate for helping, or at least guiding, is pretty good because we have a lot of different resources."[8] In addition to helping accelerate growth for their start-ups, Tim also believes the global presence provides the opportunity for his limited partners to get exposure to a broader set of opportunities, thereby leading to stronger returns potential.

There is not necessarily one right answer to these two models—the more locally focused VC or the global brand with geographic distribution. In truth, VC firms are extensions of their founders and leaders and pursue the strategy that best fits them and their culture. This preference extends to another distinction between VC firms—the particular phase of a company's growth they like to invest in.

Stage Experts: Coming in Early and Failing Cheap

Different venture capitalists have different perspectives as to when they like to enter into a business. Many VCs like to invest in the "early-stage" waters—small or not-yet-operating companies where they can get the highest percentage of

---

8. You can read more about Tim's perspective at his blog: www.theriskmaster.blogspot.com.

ownership ("I invested three million in two guys and a dog," one VC bragged to me, without revealing whether the dog also went to MIT). Others prefer to have a large amount of assets under management and invest in much bigger deals, in companies that are in relatively later stages of their development (although still considered start-ups).

The math for the later-stage strategy is simple and compelling. The more assets a VC firm has under management, the more fee income it earns. However, if the goal is to build a VC fund with over $1 billion under management, it's hard to write checks smaller than $10 million to $20 million per deal. The deals that have enough mass to absorb a large amount of capital tend to be later-stage opportunities. Yet the data show that the highest rate of return opportunities—the ones that earn you ten times or more your initial investment—lie in the early-stage deals, also known as Series A. These early-stage companies usually want to raise four to six million dollars, and often from more than one firm in order to not have a single point of dependency.

And so here's the VC conundrum: whether to focus on early-stage investments, where the risks are higher, the potential returns larger, but the fund size—and thus fee income—is smaller, or on later-stage deals where the risks are lower, the fees fatter, but the opportunities for tenfold returns are much rarer. VCs make these choices often as a matter of personal preference and as a reflection of their own interests and passion.

Founded in 2005, First Round Capital is an example of a fund that has decided to stay small and focus on the very early stage. With offices in San Francisco and outside of Philadelphia, First Round likes to write small checks in each round of financing, typically in the range of $250,000 to $1 million. Because they specialize in Internet-based businesses, they are able to make small investments and generally can avoid being heavily diluted as they would in capital-intensive companies, such as a biotechnology or semiconductor start-up. Howard Morgan, co-founder and general partner at First Round, explained to me how they developed their model. "We were the first ones to do seed-stage investing professionally. We had seen what the angels did, and we thought it was a little cumbersome. We also knew from experience how the venture model worked, where you couldn't afford to fail. The key to our strategy is failing cheap. The one lesson that I would say for all entrepreneurs is, 'If you're going to fail, fail quick and cheap.' There's no stigma in failing that way. But if you blow a hundred million bucks, big stigma."

Howard Morgan

Howard is an unusual VC in that he remains an active investor at the age of sixty-three (or "3F in Hex," he pointed out to me in a typically geeky, mathematical reference). Howard has an active, eclectic mind. He reads 180 books a year (and catalogs them on his laptop), does three crossword puzzles a day, and has an IQ of over 150. At one point in 1999, he sat on nine public boards and has been an investor in some big wins, including CitySearch, eToys, and Overture, which was acquired by Yahoo! for $1.6 billion in 2003. The incredibly high "clock speed" at which he and his co-founder, Josh Kopelman (who is also an ex-entrepreneur turned VC), are able to operate

allows them to track their portfolio of over a hundred companies and leverage the help of their co-investors to actively manage and monitor the investments. With their current fund of
$125 million spread out across so many portfolio companies,
the First Round team argues they get some advantages over
their competition because their broad set of investments gives
them insight into more markets and exposure to more interesting people. Whether their returns will be superior in the long
run to a firm that makes more concentrated bets is irrelevant
to the entrepreneur. Finding the right fit for their particular
fund-raising needs is what really matters to the entrepreneur.

The Question of Size: Large Bets Require Large Funds

When describing their funds VCs love to brag about how much
capital they have under management. "We have five gazillion
dollars under management," sniffed one VC at a cocktail party
looking down at his poor brethren, "and you guys have how
much?"

But does VC fund size really matter to the ultimate customer, the entrepreneur? Is bigger actually better? I would
argue size does matter, but perhaps not in the way that you
might think. The VC's fund size matters because it is an indicator that the VC's goals are aligned with the entrepreneur's.
A bit of history illuminates this point.

Silicon Valley–based Kleiner Perkins, one of the most successful VC firms in history, had a consistency to their fund
sizes in the 1980s and early 1990s. In 1982, they raised a $150
million fund (their third) and in 1986 another $150 million.
In 1989, you guessed it, another $150 million. And then in

1992, $173 million. Another modest increase, to $225 million, occurred in 1994.

Then, something odd happened. Beginning in the late 1990s, the Kleiner fund sizes suddenly increased markedly, and in 2000 they raised a $625 million fund. Other firms were even more aggressive during that brief five-year period. With the rush to raise bigger and bigger funds in the midst of the bubble, there was even a moment where VC partnerships argued with their limited partners that they needed to have a $1 billion fund in order to stay competitive as a top-tier firm.

What caused this fund size inflation? In short, the Internet-fueled NASDAQ bubble. From 1996 to 1999, VCs began to see exit valuations with multibillion-dollar potential, not just hundreds of millions of dollars potential. And so rather than deploy $100 million to $200 million over three or four years into start-ups at a clip of $5 to $10 million at a time, they tried to invest $1 to $2 billion over the same period by forcing $25 to $50 million at a time into their companies. And we all know how that movie ended.

With the burst of the technology bubble in 2000 and 2001, things obviously have changed. Or have they? After all, the more capital under management VCs have, the more money they make in fees. So, the natural incentive for many is to keep fund sizes large, and therefore fees large, even if the fundamentals do not support it.

Kleiner Perkins cut their post-bubble fund, raised in 2004, to $400 million—smaller than their 2000 fund, but still nearly three times what they raised in their first few decades as a firm. And then the 2008 fund was up to $700 million. Perhaps they believe the 2012–2016 exit potential for today's start-ups is three times what it was in the early to mid-1990s. The extra fee income undoubtedly helps give them extra room to support rock star advisers like Al Gore and Colin Powell, who in turn help their portfolio companies make valuable connections at the top of important business and government organizations.

To be fair, the pattern I've just described has played out throughout the industry, not just at Kleiner Perkins. And, of course, anyone would have been thrilled to have been an investor in the Kleiner Perkins fund that invested in Google, no matter how large it was. The point is that many funds have gotten very large, perhaps altering their strategy and the kinds of deals that are in their "sweet spot."

So why should an entrepreneur care about the size of a firm's fund? As we'll see in the next chapter, a critical thing for entrepreneurs when fund-raising is to find a firm that's going to be a good fit with their capital profile. After all, if VCs force too much money onto entrepreneurs, it has numerous negative effects, including more ownership dilution for the entrepreneur and a higher valuation bar required to make their VCs happy. On the other hand, not having deep-pocketed investors means there's a risk of entrepreneurs getting caught short just at the moment when a few extra million might be needed to get to the next level. Thus, the Goldilocks Rule applies to VCs and fund size: not too big, and not too small, but just right for your company and its capital requirements.

How much capital does a VC firm really want to put in each company? The marketing materials may say one thing (I once heard a VC claim they would do deals from $50,000 to $50 million), but the reality is that every firm has a sweet spot and if you as an entrepreneur are in it, you're better off than if you're not. The nature of that sweet spot comes down to the size of their current fund, not their total capital under management, and an entrepreneur should always ask about this.

The size of a VC fund influences the strategy and focus of the firm. It's an obvious observation that big funds are interested in bigger deals. But there are some rules of thumb that can help entrepreneurs translate the size of the VC fund to provide insight into the kinds of deals the firm is most likely to do.

If you're an entrepreneur with a start-up idea looking to raise $3 million to $6 million dollars, then a firm with roughly $50 million in capital per general partner is the right fit for you. But if you're looking to raise $20 million, this firm is clearly too small. And if you find yourself talking to a firm with $100 million in capital per general partner, then seeking a $3 million investment will most likely be a fruitless quest. Or you'll end up in the lamentable situation of becoming a "training wheels" investment for a freshly minted VC with an MBA on which the ink has yet to dry rather than a real investment for a senior general partner.

An early-stage firm would typically allocate about $50 million per general partner, which is what we have done at Flybridge Capital Partners, where we have five general partners investing out of our third fund of $280 million and would typically allocate about $50 million per general partner. This allows each of us to lead an investment in four to six companies over the three-year life of a fund, with $8 million to $12 million allocated per company. Usually at least half of this investment amount would be reserved for future rounds of financing, so $2 million to $8 million might be the initial investment, with another $5 million to $10 million reserved for follow-on financings—a common profile for firms with $50 million per general partner.

Later-stage VC firms prefer more capital under management because they look to deploy $10 million to $20 million per company. These funds might have as much as $100 million per partner. Take, for example, Baltimore-based JMI Equity, a well-regarded later-stage or expansion-stage investment firm that took DoubleClick private and then later sold it to Google for a handsome $3.1 billion.

JMI's 2008 fund of $600 million is being deployed by five general partners, or $120 million per partner. JMI invested in a later-stage round in one of our portfolio companies, a common pattern where early-stage venture capital firms will invest in the first round or two and then later-stage firms will invest after the company has gained revenue traction and established a more mature business model. When two VC firms with different fund sizes and investment strategies are co-investors in the same company, it yields a natural tension. The early-stage VC is typically looking to deploy less capital and the later-stage VC is typically looking to deploy more (e.g., through new product investments, international expansion, or acquisitions).

So, the size of a VC fund really does matter. And, as an entrepreneur, you want to do all you can to find that "just right" fit.

FEES AND CARRY: HOW THE VC MAKES MONEY

"If you want to really understand the VC business it's pretty simple," an old VC intoned to me wisely, "just follow the carry." I didn't really understand what he meant, until I entered the business and learned how VCs—both the firm and the individual—make money. Let me step back for a moment here to explain it to you.

The first thing to understand is just what "carry" is, and why VCs are so eager to get one. VC firms charge management fees, and partners in a VC firm draw salaries from these fees. But the potential for really big money lies in the "carried interest," that is, the percentage of profits—usually in the 20 to 25 percent range—that a VC fund earns if their fund performs well.

So what's the VC business model? Raise a fund, get paid 2 to 2.5 percent annually in fees to manage that fund, cover salaries and expenses, and make investments that you hope will generate large capital gains. When those returns are actually generated (e.g., because the portfolio company has a successful sale or IPO), the VC funds typically get their carried interest in the capital gains.

Let's walk through a typical example to see how carry is calculated. Let's say there's a $150 million fund with three general partners with 2 percent in annual fees and 20 percent in carried interest. The firm takes in $3 million in annual revenue and after paying for rent, support staff, associates, travel, et cetera, the three partners might take $400,000 to $500,000 each in salary. If the fund returns two times the capital, or

$300 million, over the ten-year life of the fund, then $150 million is considered capital gains. The VCs get 20 percent of that amount, or $30 million in carry, to be divided up between the partners according to who has how much of the carried interest (a very sensitive division, the implications of which I'll cover in a moment). If the fund doesn't generate any capital gains, the VCs get nothing beyond their salaries paid out of the annual revenue. Because VC funds are treated as separate economic entities, once the VCs have finished investing in a particular fund, they need to raise another one from their limited partners.

Funds do have long shelf lives—typically ten to twelve years—because the companies they invest in usually do not achieve liquidity for five to seven years. So the initial investment period of three or four years in which the fund is deployed is really the start-up phase during which the new investments are made. The harvest phase of the fund is over the next five to ten years when the investments mature and are sold or liquidated by going public. Thus, VC funds are often layered on top of each other. For example, we raised our second fund in 2005 ($180 million) and our third fund in 2008 ($280 million). A few years later, we are still managing the portfolio company investments from Fund 2 (and even Fund 1—raised in 2002) but, at the same time, we are making new investments out of Fund 3. Thus, both fee income and carry opportunity from multiple funds are gradually harvested year by year.

Note that associates and principals don't typically have carry. Junior partners with small slivers of carry (perhaps having one or two of the twenty "carry points") are usually supervised by senior partners who closely oversee the diligence and decision-making process. If the partners themselves are not on an equal footing in terms of carried interest, an individual partner may not be able to "speak for the firm" when it's time to make tough decisions about follow-on rounds and M&A transactions. Even the most senior partners within a firm still need to get to consensus across the partnership. That said, when your "deal champion" (i.e., the investment professional that is advocating your case within the partnership) is a subordinate within the VC firm, it can be a harder and longer process than when the deal champion is one of the senior partners.

One of the most fundamental choices a VC firm makes is how to divide up the compensation among the partnership. For example, Benchmark is a well-regarded firm in Silicon Valley that is famous for being an equal partnership, a fact that is even marketed on their website ("Every full-time partner is equal in terms of contribution and compensation"). At Flybridge, we decided to emulate the Benchmark model. We founded the firm as peers and felt it was important to maintain a culture of equal voice, equal pay. Other firms have more of a hierarchical structure, with senior partners owning more carry and thus more of the decision-making power than junior partners.

I would encourage entrepreneurs to ask the VCs with whom they're talking how the carry is divided within the partnership. It is a reasonable question to ask and will provide revealing insights into the partnership's culture and division of decision-making authority. After all, VCs are always asking entrepreneurs how they divide up the founding equity, as a mechanism to understand the values and priorities of the founding team. Turnabout is fair play.

IT'S NOT (JUST) ABOUT THE RETURN:
IT'S ALSO A MARRIAGE (KIND OF)

I hope you now have a sense of the character of VCs, the various types of VC firms, and how they make their money. It's also important to consider VCs as individuals (and complex ones) who are driven as much by emotion, instinct, gut feel, and personal taste as they are by rational analysis and cold hard data.

Not all business areas are a fit for all VC firms. There are some businesses that just don't interest certain VCs. Tim Draper of DFJ, for example, says that his fund looks at all the business plans that come in and weeds out the "no-gos" quickly. "The business plan is our starting point. I don't take phone calls because there are just too many of them, but I have time to read plans. My partners also have time and my analysts and associates go through every one. I don't let them *not* go through every one, because they might have a bias, but the business plan still might be good. I'm always looking for the upside. I think about how the business would go if everything worked the way the entrepreneur wanted it to work. That's what I care about. So we go through every single business plan, and my associates say, 'Oh, this is a dry cleaner,' and I say, 'Okay, I'm not going to do a dry cleaner.' Or, 'This is a metal shop,' and I say, 'I'm not going to do a metal shop.' Restaurant? Probably won't do a restaurant. But, if it's a serious business that fits our model in one way or another, we'll probably bring the entrepreneur in."

In addition to the business area, the personality and character of the entrepreneur and the chemistry with the VC also matter, as we'll discuss more in Chapter 3 (The Pitch) and Chapter 4 (Catching the Bus). "Getting venture and financing is like a marriage, but one that you know is not supposed to be for a lifetime," Reid Hoffman said. "So it's really important to carefully select the individual that you're partnering with in creating the business. And before I came up with that romance parallel, I just thought it was kind of an instrument. You get money and then you have a board member, and it's more of a mechanical thing. Money is obviously fundamental, but if you don't partner well with the person, then it's potential death."

But before you have the privilege to select your ideal VC partner, you have to convince them that you can make them money. That's where the pitch comes in.

3

THE PITCH: BEING THE ONE
IN THREE HUNDRED

Now we get to the moment when the entrepreneur presents himself and his business idea to a member of the VC club. This sales effort is known as "the pitch." Many entrepreneurs are not naturally very good at this critical process, and many actively hate it, but they *can* learn—as I did.

The pitch can come in many forms. Sometimes it's twenty PowerPoint slides that lay out your idea and plan for global domination. Other times it's the five-minute "elevator pitch" that you can deliver on the fly or on the phone to entice someone to spend more time with you. For the entrepreneur, it is the most critical, salient expression of their business idea encapsulated into a tight summary to convey credibility and confidence. For the VC, it's a process of rapidly sifting through a lot of information about people, markets, and technologies to find the veritable needle in the haystack. Based on the experience at our firm and the dozens of VCs I interviewed for the book, I calculate that VCs invest in only one out of every three hundred companies to which they are exposed. As I said, they're looking for a needle in the haystack of deals.

I made my first major VC pitch during my second week on the job at Upromise. My partner, Michael Bronner, and I flew out to California to meet with John Doerr and his partners at Kleiner Perkins Caulfield & Byers, generally known as Kleiner Perkins. John Doerr is one of the most famous VCs in history and considered the "center of gravity in the Internet," according to Jeff Bezos, founder of Amazon.com. After graduating from Harvard Business School, John went to work for Intel in 1974, just as the company was bringing out the 8080 Microprocessor (essentially the first microchip). He went on to become an amazingly successful VC, investing at an early stage in Amazon, Google, Sun, and Intuit, among others. I was excited to meet this Silicon Valley legend.

It was not my first time visiting the nondescript low-rise office buildings on famous Sand Hill Road in the heart of Silicon Valley, but it was my first time doing it with hat in hand, trying to raise money and delivering the pitch. When we arrived, the receptionist and support staff made us feel at home offering cold drinks, fresh fruit, magazines, and newspapers— all with warm smiles and welcoming words. I later learned that Kleiner Perkins, like many of the best VC firms, instructs their support staff to treat entrepreneurs like superstars rather than peons begging for money (which we were).

Michael and I were ushered into the "fishbowl," the glass-enclosed conference room where the partner meetings are held. Although we were a bit intimidated to be in front of the entire Kleiner Perkins partnership (which, in addition to

Doerr, included other VC legends, like Sun co-founder Vinod Khosla), the pitch started off well. We articulated our vision: to help millions of families save money for college by harnessing the billions of dollars spent by major consumer companies on promotional incentives (miles, points, rebates). We talked about our past experiences in helping build a major consumer marketing services company (Michael) and a leading Internet commerce company (me) and the fact that this new start-up would be a blend of the two. The Kleiner Perkins partners listened politely and patiently. I thought things were going reasonably well.

Then, on slide 17, John Doerr went to work on us. "What are the revenue drivers that would bring the break-even point forward another six months?" he asked, looking intently at one of the PowerPoint slides of our pitch document. Michael turned to me as if I should know the answer. With only a week under my belt, I froze and looked blankly back at him. "And why do you figure year-four gross margins at 88 percent," John continued, without waiting for a response to the first question, "instead of at 65 percent, as you show for year two?" He looked up with a penetrating stare. I racked my brain for a cogent answer and came up with something. I honestly can't remember what I said. Obviously it wasn't totally convincing. John and the other partners around the table smelled fear. They asked a dozen more killer questions. We stumbled ahead and answered as best we could. Finally, it was over.

Later that day, one of the Kleiner Perkins partners called me to inform us of their decision. "We decided we're going to invest in you and join in this financing," he said. "We love the vision and are convinced that it's a huge market opportunity.

But I have to say, for a couple of guys who have stellar reputations for being strong executors, you didn't really have your arms around the financial details." I had prepared for the pitch as best I could in the brief time I had. I knew many of the elements of the business plan cold, but he was right. I didn't know the underlying drivers of the financials as well as I should have. I had assumed that Michael did, but he, in turn, assumed I did. We were so busy scrambling to get the business off the ground that we hadn't invested the time to analyze, rehearse, and practice our pitch as much as we should have. Although we were lucky to get funded by Kleiner and other great firms as a result of our compelling idea and strong backgrounds, at that moment, I resolved never to walk into a pitch, or any meeting with a VC, without knowing every number and every detail inside and out. And, as a VC, that is what I have come to expect of every entrepreneur who pitches me.

THE PERILS OF THE PITCH

Perhaps it shouldn't surprise me, considering that early experience of my own, but very few entrepreneurs have a well-informed understanding of the importance of the pitch, how to get in front of the right firm, and how to make a presentation the VC partners will find irresistible.

Mastering the pitch process is essential to getting venture capital funding. Sometimes an entrepreneur will hook an investor with a single pitch, but it's more usual for him to have to make many pitches—sometimes dozens over a period of several months—before he connects with a VC firm and secures the level of interest he is looking for. Plenty of entrepreneurs pitch their hearts out and never get an offer.

It's not surprising that entrepreneurs get a little cranky about the process. After being rejected time and time again, they start to think of VCs as fundamentally risk-averse or lacking in the judgment and vision needed to recognize their once-in-a-lifetime investment opportunity. One of our portfolio CEOs, a successful serial entrepreneur, pitched thirty venture capital firms before getting funding from us for his venture. In his opinion, the twenty-nine who turned him down were idiots. Because we wrote the check, he thinks we're brilliant. Meanwhile, the other twenty-nine VCs probably think we're idiots for backing him. Go figure.

In my experience, there is usually a good, logical reason why venture capitalists say no and the entrepreneur fails to get his project funded. After all, venture capitalists are in the business of investing in start-ups. That's what their investors pay them to do, and it's the reason they get out of bed every morning. They want to hear pitches and fund great businesses. The problem they have is that most projects just don't meet their selection criteria. There's either not enough upside potential or there's too much risk, the entrepreneur doesn't really have the right qualifications, there's no chemistry between the entrepreneur and the VC, or the business just doesn't get the VC sufficiently fired up. Passion for a market, a technology, and the qualities of the entrepreneur plays a big role.

The pitch may not be everything, but it counts for a lot, and if you get it wrong, it counts against you.

Scope Out the Firm

I have heard some people argue that the VC pitch process is analogous to dating, but to me it's more like car shopping. Most people date in a serial fashion before they find the right person (at least that's the old-fashioned way in which I operated before I got married), but they shop for cars in parallel—checking out multiple dealers and multiple brands before making a choice. Similarly, entrepreneurs should explore different types of venture capital firms, different firms of the same type, and even different partners within a firm before settling on the ones they want to approach, pitch to, and, ultimately, work with. Before they make the decision to buy, consumers have to decide whether they want to see and be seen in that particular car every day for the next five to ten years—if they want their personal brand associated with, say, a BMW 7 Series or a Toyota Prius. Similarly, the entrepreneur needs to feel comfortable being associated with and working alongside a particular VC.

Smart entrepreneurs take a strategic approach, assessing the general kind of VC firm they should select to pitch. As discussed in Chapter 2, the considerations should include distinguishing between local or global firms, early- or late-stage experts, industry specialists, and firms with large or small funds. It means finding out about the operating and investing background of the firm. What kinds of deals have they done? Have they made any investments that are similar to your start-up? What kind of businesses do they like? What business areas do they *never* invest in? (In the case of DFJ's Tim Draper, obviously, metal shops and dry cleaners.) How well have the companies in their portfolio done? Which partner at the firm did which deals? What are the partners like to work with—how well do they reference with other entrepreneurs who have worked with them?

Scoping out VC firms also means learning as many details as you can about their current situation. It's important to know where the firm is within its own business cycle. Where are they in their new fund cycle? Did the firm just raise a fund and therefore has plenty of fresh capital available to put to work? Or is the firm in the middle of raising a new fund, in which case the partners are too consumed with pitching limited partners to pay attention to new deals? A firm may be "sold out," as one of my VC friends likes to put it, when his firm can't do any new deals due to a lack of available funds. If the firm is between funds, it means that no matter how much they like your idea, they don't have the checkbook to support it. Even mundane considerations, such as the time of year, matter in the pitch process. For example, VCs are said to be notorious for slowing down over the summer and having problems coordinating schedules and convening the full partnership to make investment decisions at that time. When you look at the data, however, this may in fact be a VC legend more than reality.[9]

The VC partnership may be affected by other factors—if they have recently sold off a company for a big gain or, conversely, shut down a project. If the fund performance has been less stellar than they had hoped, VCs may get very selective, looking for a few short-term, relatively safe, later-stage investments to improve the fund's performance during the remain-

---

9. See my blog post "Do VCs Take the Summer Off?" at http://bostonvcblog.typepad .com/vc/2009/06/do-vcs-take-the-summer-off-entrepreneurs-say-yes-the-data-says-no .html.

der of its life. Conversely, if the fund's performance has been very strong, partners may be bursting with confidence and less risk-averse. They may be willing to try to "swing for the fences" with the final few investments, taking a bigger chance for a higher potential reward, knowing that even a lackluster result won't kill the overall performance of the fund.

It is not just the brand and attributes of the particular VC firm that matter to the entrepreneur, but also the particular partner who would become the board member and business partner in the venture. He is the one you are stuck with on the late-night conference calls and 7:00 A.M. emergency board meetings. You need to investigate whether the partner you're particularly interested in working with has any capacity for new deals and for adding companies to his portfolio. Partners typically sit on the boards of the companies they have funded, and there is a limit to how many boards a partner can handle. At the time of this writing, I currently sit on eight boards. Tim Draper at DFJ is on six, and Fred Wilson of Union Square Ventures is on seven. Ten is usually the maximum, with five to ten the norm. So, if the partner at the VC firm you're interested in sits on more than ten boards, it's unlikely he'll be interested in taking on any more commitments, never mind able to devote the time and attention you want and need. Further, most partners don't like to do more than two or three deals a year (the average is one to two), so if he's recently taken on a few new deals, he may be loath to start yet another new effort, never mind convince his partnership that he has the bandwidth to take on a new one.

Arrange for a Warm Introduction

Once you have identified the firms and particular partners you think would be a good fit, put some care into how you approach them.

I know this sounds absurd, but many entrepreneurs do what the most inexperienced college grad would do when looking for a first job: They try to get a meeting with a cold call or email. They put together a list of the names of VC firms, send out a standard email containing a description (usually too long) of their beloved project, and ask for a pitch meeting. "I will be in touch soon in hopes that we can find a mutually convenient time to meet. All the best . . ." They don't know the venture capitalist personally and often don't do enough homework about the partners or their firm and, therefore, have little knowledge of the kinds of projects the VCs might be interested in, how large their fund is, what businesses they have funded in the past, or anything else about them.

This approach does not work. Of the nearly fifty companies that we at Flybridge Capital have invested in over our eight-year history, not one of them came in cold. In fact, I polled a number of my VC colleagues on the topic, and we estimate that the odds of getting a pitch meeting from a cold email are 500 to 1, at best. The odds of actually receiving funding from a cold email: 50,000 to 1. You are better off playing the lottery.

Remember, VCs are skilled networkers. Via LinkedIn, Facebook, and Twitter, they connect to the thousands of entrepreneurs and companies they meet or that their fellow VCs have invested in. The people they don't know they can easily get to with a single email or phone call to a mutual acquaintance or by seeking them out at an industry conference in Silicon Valley, New York, or Boston. So when an entrepreneur makes a cold approach to a VC, it marks him as an outsider. The guy doesn't know *anybody*? He can't find a better way to get to me? He may look clueless about this most basic aspect of deal making.

"Venture capital is a tiny industry," said Patricia Nakache, a general partner at Trinity Ventures, a Silicon Valley–based early-stage firm that was the first institutional investor in Starbucks. "It definitely helps to be a known quantity. It's all about mutual connections."

Patricia Nakache

Patricia, one of the few female VCs, is about as connected as one can get. Her father, a PhD in nuclear engineering, worked for a consulting firm and managed projects all over the world. Growing up, Patricia lived in New York, Los Angeles, Paris, Brussels, and Washington. She went to Harvard as an undergraduate, studied physics and chemistry, then joined McKinsey & Company right after she graduated in 1986. She left McKinsey to earn her MBA at Stanford and then returned to McKinsey in Silicon Valley. She spent several years there, during which time she got married, had a child, and started freelancing for *Fortune* magazine—writing stories about entrepreneurs and venture capitalists and startups. While at *Fortune*, she interviewed some of the partners at Trinity, many of whom she had met through other mutual connections. She got interested in the VC world and, in 1998, joined the firm as a venture consultant. She later became a general partner.

Few entrepreneurs will have the breadth of connections that Patricia does, and no VC would expect them to. What's important for the entrepreneur, especially the first-time entrepreneur, is to understand just how well connected the partners around the table really are, and how much they rely on their networks for information and deals.

This does not mean that if you don't know anybody, you can't make connections that will help you. Networking tools, such as Reid Hoffman's LinkedIn, as well as old-fashioned Rolodex-building activities, like attending relevant conferences and mining various alumni networks, should allow any determined entrepreneur to get a warm introduction.

Venture capitalists admire tenacity and resourcefulness—all qualities that an entrepreneur can and should exhibit from the first email, phone call, or handshake with a VC. Think about China, with over a billion citizens and millions of aspiring entrepreneurs, yet its VC community is less than one-tenth the size of the one in the United States. I asked my friend Quan Zhou, co-founder and managing director of IDG-Accel China, one of the country's leading venture capital firms (profiled in Chapter 7), how he assesses the quality of the entrepreneur from the strangers who come in over the transom. He noted, "People always send me an email with a business plan, but the good ones establish some connection to me. That's the number-one test—How aggressive is he? If he can't find a way to get to me, how can he successfully get to customers?"

For example, when we started Upromise, Michael Bronner and I knew we wanted to get to John Doerr. We networked to him through three sources—one of my HBS professors who knew him well, a Silicon Valley CEO friend of Michael's who knew him, and a Fortune 500 CEO with whom Michael was friendly. After hearing about us from these trusted sources, even a guy as busy as John Doerr decided it was worth taking a meeting. If we had simply cold-called him, we would never have gotten in front of him. In truth, one of his younger partners took the first meeting—to screen us—before our deal progressed to the full partnership, a common technique senior VCs will use to leverage their time efficiently. Tim Draper of DFJ described his strategy as follows: "My analysts and associates look at the business plan and take the initial call. And then if it seems good to them, they will bring it back to me. Then, if it's a serious business that fits our model in one way or another, I'll say, 'I want to meet them.'"

Prepare, Be Brief, Don't Downplay the Risk

Once you have secured a pitch meeting—preferably through a warm introduction—how you conduct the pitch is crucial. As I demonstrated in the account of my Upromise pitch to Kleiner Perkins, a lack of preparation can be painful, if not fatal.

At the initial meeting, you may not get much time to state your case. At First Round Capital, you're likely to get thirty minutes, maybe another fifteen for questions. "Thirty minutes is enough to see if the passion is there," First Round Capital's Howard Morgan told me. "It's enough to get a sense of the person, to see if he knows what he's doing." As DFJ's Tim Draper put it to me bluntly: "If I can't figure it out in thirty minutes, then I'm an idiot, and we won't invest."

It goes without saying that the first fifteen minutes of your time allotment is critically important to establish credibility and relevance. I did a blog post a few years ago that got a lot of feedback from entrepreneurs called "VCs Blink."[10] In it, I remind entrepreneurs that VCs are like most human beings in how they process information. As Malcolm Gladwell's best-selling book *Blink* observed, we all make quick judgments based on first impressions. Thus, I advise entrepreneurs to pause fifteen minutes into the meeting and check in with the VCs to see if they think the pitch is interesting and has a chance of going anywhere. As Union Square's Fred Wilson observed wryly, "I usually give people an hour. But I think that's actually a mistake. If you're fifteen minutes into a pitch, and you know you're not interested, the next forty-five minutes are brutal."

If things go well in that first pitch, you may be asked back for a second meeting, which usually takes place after the partners have discussed your pitch, declared it interesting, and have some follow-up questions and concerns. "We come out of our first meeting, and we have some specific drill-down areas that we have questions about," Patricia Nakache of Trinity Ventures said. "So, we set up another session to talk about those issues. What impresses me and my partners is when the entrepreneur comes in and nails the answers. They show that they have prepared. They're saying, 'I heard you.' They put together a specific analysis that responds to our questions. When that happens, I say, 'Okay, this team turns on a dime, they understand issues, they know how to address them.' It makes me

---

10. See "VCs Blink" at http://bostonvcblog.typepad.com/vc/2005/09/vcs_blink.html.

confident that when there's an issue, these guys will get right
to the heart of it."

Many entrepreneurs make the mistake of playing down the
risk of their venture in the pitch for capital. Venture capitalists
know there are risks involved in every start-up. They want to
know what they are, and they want to know that the entrepreneur knows what they are. Paranoia kept Christoph Westphal
of Sirtris from overpromising on his vision. "I'd say to the VCs,
'Look, the odds that I'm right are less than ten percent. But
if I am right, this is *really* big.'" In a later round of financing,
Christoph told one of his investors, "'Odds are you're going
to lose this money.' [Ironically,] that's what gave him comfort
with me."

Reid Hoffman, founder and chairman of LinkedIn, is ada-
mant about not overpromising. "As an entrepreneur, you're
visualizing success at this random new thing that you're trying
to do. You say to the venture capitalist, 'I'm going to be able to
do this, this, and this.' But you're gambling into the future, you
don't really know that you'll get there. So if the venture guys
look back and say, 'Hey, it didn't happen the way you said it
would,' you're like, 'Oops.'" Many VCs joke that there are two
phrases you always hear in every pitch: "This is the only (or
last) money we will ever need" and "These projections are very
conservative." I would estimate that out of the five thousand
business plans I've reviewed in the last eight years as a VC, only
1-2 percent performed better than the numbers in the plan.

Reid's advice is: don't oversell. "I've learned the hard way
that it's better to say, 'Look, this is a gamble. It's a risk. I believe
I can do it successfully, but it hasn't been done yet, so we're

going to see if it plays out.' That's better than articulating it as 'We'll succeed.' Because if you fail, you get grumpiness from your venture people."

You really don't want that.

A Good Pitch Overcomes a Lot of Weirdness

◆ When an entrepreneur has a good idea and makes a strong pitch, the venture capitalist can overlook minor and not-so-minor annoyances.

David Hornik of August Capital regaled me with this anecdote highlighting one CEO's eccentricity. "We were being pitched by a group of entrepreneurs. The CEO had passed the torch to another member of the team and was not part of the conversation at the moment. He proceeded to take out his nail clipper and cut his nails. It was stunning. The boldest thing I've ever seen." And guess what? August Capital funded them.

Fred Wilson, when he was with his previous firm, Flatiron Ventures, had a memorable pitch experience with a different outcome. "In 1999 or 2000, a guy came into our office to pitch an idea for a new company," Fred told me. "He brought his dog, Sophie, with him. She's one of those big, buzz-cut dogs. We go into the conference room, which had a floor-to-ceiling window in the main office area, where a number of people were working. The entrepreneur and I sit down, Sophie lies down, and he starts pitching me. We're just getting going, maybe five minutes in, when something happens out in the main office. Somebody makes a quick move, and there's a loud noise. Sophie leaps up, and runs, *bam*, right into the window, hard, and she's knocked out cold. The entrepreneur jumps up, 'Sophie, Sophie, oh my Sophie!' just like a little kid. He wasn't married, and this dog was his baby. Finally, the dog lifts her head. The guy says, 'I can't continue.' He picks her up, *boom*, he's gone, meeting's over. I never heard from him on that deal again."

GETTING PAST NO: WHAT DOES A VC *WANT*?

Now, what might be going through the mind of the VC who funds an entrepreneur who is so bold—shall I say rude?—as to clip his fingernails in the middle of the pitch meeting or who puts his beloved dog ahead of his need for money?

What does the VC *want*? What is he looking for?

The process by which VCs consider deals—known as processing the "deal flow"—is one of the most fascinating things about the VC business. In most VC firms, the deal flow process is most evident when partners gather to discuss which deals they will pursue and why, and which ones they'll pass on. This conversation usually takes place in "the Monday morning meeting," which is the meeting of the VC firm's partners held each week at their offices. It is dreaded by entrepreneurs, because the thumbs-up or thumbs-down call usually comes in right after this meeting has adjourned.

How to best manage their deal flow is a quandary for the VC. A VC wants to see every interesting start-up that is happening, particularly those led by proven entrepreneurs. The more deals a VC sees, the more likely he will have the opportunity to select a high-quality deal in which to invest. And there's a secondary benefit to having high-volume, high-quality deal flow as well. By looking at as many deals as possible, VCs become smarter investors—learning a little something from every deal seen, and becoming more adept at detecting useful patterns.

The volume of possible deals is so great, however, that no partner can review all the business plans, let alone fund all the companies that might be worthy. A VC with a healthy deal flow may get an opportunity to review as many as three hundred to five hundred deals per year. Most "active" VCs—those who will join the board of the company in which they invest—typically have capacity to do no more than one or two deals a year. "Passive" VCs—those who may come in at a later stage, take a smaller ownership stake, and don't join the board—have greater deal capacity but still only do three or four deals annually per partner.

So for VCs, managing their deal flow is a matter of examining as many deals as possible, winnowing them down to a manageable number as efficiently as possible, and following a process of evaluation that is as effective as possible. It is essentially a sales process, with a bit of mutual selling (and evaluating) by both the VC and the entrepreneur, and it usually proceeds through a number of stages before the deal is closed.

As I've mentioned, typically a deal flows from an initial meeting (a half hour to an hour) to a follow-up meeting (one or two hours, when more specific issues are addressed) to the light due diligence phase. This phase often involves a visit by the VC to the entrepreneur's place of business (if he has one), as well as placing a few calls to references to get some background on the entrepreneur (many VCs will simply thumb a quick email on their BlackBerry to a mutual friend to do a quick sniff test on the entrepreneur: "Jane Smith—backable or . . . . ?"). The VC will also consult an expert or two in the industry to get some perspective on the business. If all proceeds well, the investment opportunity will proceed to the next phase, where the VC will have some or all of their partners meet with the firm while in parallel conducting heavy due diligence, which includes extensive market research, customer references, an analysis of the competition, technical evaluation, and a more complete checkup of personal references of the management team. The final stage involves getting all partners in the firm to meet the company (yes, on Monday morning), buy in to the investment decision, and prepare the term sheet, which is discussed in Chapter 4.

At the end of this evaluation process, different VC firms have different policies when it comes to making the final decision whether or not to invest. Some firms, such as Flybridge, explicitly vote on deals and score them across a number of dimensions (e.g., quality of team, size of market, nature of technology and competition, attractiveness of deal terms). Like many firms, we have a unanimous policy—all partners must affirmatively support a new investment and any one partner can veto it. Other firms allow individual partners or a pair of partners to push a deal through past their colleagues' objections. Tim Draper's DFJ operates this way, and he explains: "I want the positive vote to have the power. If it's a bad investment, we lose our money one time. But we can make a thousand times our money if we get that weird one that happens once in a while."

Obviously, most of the deals that enter the process get nixed along the way. I have come to think of the world of VC deal flow as a Dr. Seussian "Land of No." Imagine a crazy conveyor belt running through the VC office, overloaded with packages representing start-up companies in a variety of different sizes and wrappings. Standing before the conveyor belt is a row of VC Weenies—fresh-faced, horn-rimmed, thirty-something MBAs in their customary khakis and blue button-down shirts. The Weenies inspect the packages as they roll by, picking them up, shaking them, peering inside them, holding them up to the light. "Here's a Blue-Horned Skreet. Should we invest in that?" one asks. *"No!"* the others say. "I have here a Buck-Toothed Blarg," says another Weenie, waving a bright-looking package. "What say you all?" Comes the inevitable reply, *"No!"* A third Weenie rattles a techie-looking package. "This comes from an MIT PhD with a wireless start-up! Shall we green-light it?" The Weenies pause for just a millisecond before we hear their blistering, *"No! No!* A thousand times *no!"*

And, by the way, some VCs are pretty rude when they are not interested in your start-up. The common bad behavior you will hear entrepreneurs complain about is the VC playing with his iPhone or BlackBerry during the entire meeting (many have both). And perhaps most frustrating of all is when the VC doesn't respond to the entrepreneur's calls and emails, not even deigning to take the time to officially turn down the opportunity or provide constructive feedback. Although this bad behavior is inexcusable, one of my partners likes to quote from the Jennifer Aniston movie *He's Just Not That Into You* when counseling entrepreneurs to not take it personally, but to take the hint and move on.

In order for a venture capitalist to say yes to your deal in this Land of No, she is looking for a certain set of characteristics that makes the plan virtually irresistible in every way and at every stage. In the next section, let's review those key characteristics that are required to overcome the VCs' propensity to say *"No."*

A Compelling Vision That Hits the Sweet Spot

First, venture capitalists, as cynical as they can sometimes get, do have a sweet spot, and they are inclined to favor deals that hit it.

Gail Goodman is president, CEO, and chairman of the email marketing firm Constant Contact. A former management consultant and marketing executive at numerous start-ups (including Open Market, where we worked together), she joined Constant Contact at a very early stage and adroitly grew it from virtually

nothing to a market leader servicing over three hundred thousand clients and, in 2007, led its successful IPO on the NASDAQ. Along the way, Gail estimates that she was rejected by over forty VCs before securing her first round of VC money and by over sixty before securing her second. Although there was some overlap between the two rounds, this means nearly one

Gail Goodman

hundred VCs were wrong to turn her down—the company currently has a market capitalization of nearly $1 billion.

"The biggest lesson I learned," Gail said, "is to get better and better at knowing whether you're in the VC sweet spot. For example, if all they do is enterprise software, and you're not in enterprise software, don't be there. Don't waste your time."

Of course, being in a particular VC's sweet spot is important but not enough. The entrepreneur has to come up with a vision, an idea, an approach that gets the venture capitalist and his partners excited. Howard Morgan at First Round Capital points to the entrepreneur's passion as a key element that gets him fired up. "Being an entrepreneur is hard work. If you're going to launch a start-up, you had better be passionate about it. And you better be able to transmit that passion." In the case of Gail Goodman and Constant Contact, the VCs who funded her bought into her vision that every small business in the world would benefit from using email as a marketing and communication channel—a vision about which she was passionate and could convey in a compelling way.

Reid Hoffman's idea about how the Internet might be harnessed to bring professional people together also caught the imagination of several VCs. You can't stop Reid when he's on a roll about the impact his start-up could have on people around the world. "LinkedIn had to do with how I think the Internet works, how it changes people's lives," observed Reid. "Everyone's a publisher, everyone has identity, and these trusted networks are going to be the things that filter signal from noise. It could completely transform recruiting, for example. [LinkedIn] will be a whole set of applications about how the right kind of business recommendations and information are found in order to make stuff happen."

The more dramatic and unrealized the vision, the more the experience and expertise of the entrepreneur come under scrutiny by the VC. "As a first-time entrepreneur, I could have never gotten LinkedIn financed," Reid confided to me. "They'd say, 'Okay, great, we see that big vision, but what's the specific thing? What's the product that works on the Internet, the features that people are going to need, the method of viral distribution?' You need to be very specific in order to raise money. So I'd say, 'Well, the specific thing is a way of connecting with other professionals, establishing a profile, and a way of doing searches.' " But in the end, the VCs cared about the people behind the idea as much as, if not more than, the idea itself.

And people are perhaps the most important attribute required in order to attract VC money.

The Right People—An Unfair Advantage

Sweet spot + compelling vision + wrong people = no funding.

It's simply not enough to find the right VC partners at the right VC firm and pitch to them your compelling vision. In addition, you and your team need to be the right team to pursue this compelling vision and bring it to life. Ideas are a dime a dozen. Having a world-class team that can uniquely execute on the ideas is golden.

Every VC asks himself at some point in the due diligence process, "What happens if a 'fast follower' comes up with the same idea, raises more money, and recruits a better team?" The entrepreneur who has a clear, unassailable competitive advantage, something I like to call an "unfair advantage," is the most compelling entrepreneur when it comes to the pitch.

In the early days at Upromise, we had two unfair advantages linked to the two key elements of the business plan. We had to convince chief marketing officers (CMOs) and CEOs to redirect billions of dollars allocated to other rewards and incentives to go toward college savings. To do this, we had the unfair advantage of having Michael Bronner as our founder and CEO. Michael had spent the last twenty years working as a marketing strategist for these same CMOs and CEOs in creating his marketing services firm, Digitas. He knew them, they knew him, and there was tremendous mutual respect and trust, enough to risk trying something new.

The second key element of our business plan was that we had to work within the complex tax code to create tax-advantaged college savings accounts that had recently been created, called

529 plans. In order to have the right to manage one of these 529 plans, now widely known as the "401(k) for college," we needed to convince a state to name us as the program manager for their plan. To create an unfair advantage here, we hired an executive from Merrill Lynch who is credited as being one of the fathers of the tax-free college savings industry. He brought us instant credibility with state treasurers and financial institutions.

Similarly, VCs are looking to back entrepreneurial teams that can effectively execute on the big vision and bring it to life. Fred Wilson of Union Square puts it, "We VCs love to invest in the serial entrepreneur who's done it before, knows the playbook, and won't make any of the rookie mistakes. And when those people come back, if they still have the fire in their belly to do it again, we're likely to say 'yes' almost every single time."

But experience cuts both ways. An entrepreneur who knows too much physics doesn't believe he can defy gravity. Many VCs prefer young founders who are incredibly brilliant and gifted even though they are inexperienced and naïve. Look at the case studies of the successful start-ups begun by college dropouts, such as Microsoft (Bill Gates), Dell (Michael Dell), and Facebook (Mark Zuckerberg). Fred Wilson's observation on Facebook is that the singular focus of the young entrepreneur is very powerful. "You have this twenty-five-year-old founder, Mark Zuckerberg, who doesn't have a wife, he doesn't have kids, he doesn't have anything in his life that's distracting him from what he's trying to do. And there's nobody saying to him, 'God damn it, take the money off the table. It's fifteen billion dollars. You should sell it now.' Instead, he's going for a hundred billion! Now that may be a stupid move or it might be a brilliant move. Only time will tell."

The powerful combination of these three forces—finding the right VC match, having a compelling vision, and assembling a uniquely strong team—can be seen in more detail with the following two case studies that we funded at Flybridge Capital Partners: Brontes and Predictive BioSciences.

A Movie, Not a Snapshot

Even when everything looks good, VCs do not like to be rushed into a decision. They prefer to see the company and team evolve over time, like a movie, as opposed to a snapshot taken at a discrete point in time. One curmudgeonly VC once instructed me, "Jeff, if an entrepreneur tries to rush you and asks for a decision before you are ready, that's VC 101: the answer is always 'no.' Do not make rushed decisions." In contrast, if a team walks into the first meeting and outlines what they plan on achieving in the next two months and then walks in two months later having achieved each of the milestones—plus two more they hadn't promised—it's very impressive to the VC.

Having learned this lesson as an entrepreneur, I have passed it along to others after becoming a venture capitalist and I know it sticks with them. When I first met Eric Paley, for example, he was a student at Harvard Business School. I was visiting a class in entrepreneurial finance, where the Upromise case was being taught. Eric approached me after the class ended. He didn't try to pitch an idea; he just asked me a simple question, "What kind of entrepreneurial mentors have you had in your career? How did you approach them?" We talked a bit, but I didn't think much of it.

Although he didn't tell me about it at the time, Eric was

Eric Paley

working on a new business plan. He had already helped found an Internet marketing company, so he had some entrepreneurial experience under his belt. Enough, in fact, that he and his partner, Micah Rosenbloom, had been invited by a team of researchers at MIT, led by Professor Doug Hart and research scientist Janos Rohaly, to visit their lab and take a look at a 3-D imaging system. The scientists wanted to find an entrepreneur to help them commercialize the system.

Eric and Micah jumped at the opportunity to team up with the MIT group to pursue an entrepreneurial initiative. "Micah and I were very pushy with Doug and Janos," Eric told me. "We said, 'Look, not all MBAs are created equal. You need somebody who actually knows what they're doing, has actually started a business before, and understands this process. And we're open to working with you, because this is really interesting.' Finally, Doug wrote us a note saying, 'We have decided to choose you because you're the most pushy, but we don't like you.'" Paley continued, "It took time to build trust on the team. The strength of the team is that we came from different backgrounds, but that was also a stylistic tension at the beginning."

A few weeks after that class, Eric called me. "I'm working on this interesting thing at MIT," he told me. At that time, their plan was to develop the 3-D imaging technology as a machine vision system for use in an industrial environment. "Sounds interesting," I said. "Why don't we meet and talk about it?"

As it turned out, I wasn't particularly excited about the

machine vision idea. I didn't think the market opportunity was large enough and easy enough to access quickly, but we had a good conversation and I got to know Eric a little better.

That was the second scene in the Eric Paley movie.

"You gave us a lot of really useful advice in that meeting," Eric later told me (and this was after I had invested in him, so he wasn't just sucking up). "And it helped us when we went out to pitch the machine vision business."

Based on the feedback they were getting and their ongoing research of the market, Eric and his partner began to question their own convictions about the opportunity. But then they got an offer for funding from a well-respected fund that had gone deep into diligence with them. "They were prepared to fund us," Eric said. "We had a 'rubber-stamp' all-partners meeting on the calendar. They told us they had not turned down a company in that meeting in over a year." But just a couple of weeks before the meeting, one of the partners called to tell Eric that he was planning to attend a machine vision conference to do a little more evaluation of the industry. "There was no way we were going to let them go to the conference and draw their own conclusions. We had to be there, too. The conference turned out to be incredibly depressing. I said to myself, 'Even I don't want to be in this industry.'"

That weekend, Eric had dinner with a dentist friend. Six months earlier, while sitting in the dentist's chair, Eric had told him about the 3-D imaging system. "What if you could scan the mouth?" Eric asked, as best he could with a mouthful of cotton and suction tubes. "Would that be useful?" At the time, the dentist didn't say much (too busy scraping away at Eric's teeth, I guess), and Eric forgot all about the conversation.

Later, at the dinner, however, the dentist asked eagerly, "So, how's that dental scanner coming along?"

Eric told him that they were working on a different use for the technology. "That's really a shame," the dentist said. "Why?" Eric asked, surprised that his friend had even remembered the conversation. "Well," said the dentist, "dental impressions are really a pain in the butt. Nobody likes them. They're inaccurate, which means that crowns come back inaccurate. Addressing that would be a game changer."

Eric and Micah spent the weekend thinking about it. At that moment, they exhibited a key entrepreneurial trait: an ability to quickly change directions and pursue a more attractive opportunity—often referred to as "the pivot." After some more research, they concluded that the dentistry application had much more promise than machine vision. A week before the final partners meeting with the VC firm, Eric called the partner and said, "We're not coming in." The partner was flabbergasted and exploded. "We are going to decide to fund you on Monday! Do you understand how irresponsible you're being?" Eric gulped. Clearly, the fact that this particular sponsoring partner, who was new to the partnership, had invested so much of his own time and reputation within the partnership affected the strength of his response. Eric was in a difficult spot. It is very tough to turn down funding when you've been rejected by thirty, forty, or fifty other VCs, and he knew he might burn a bridge and damage his relationship with the sponsoring partner. But Eric held firm. "We're going to come back to you in eight weeks with something you're going to like even better."

So Eric and Micah spent eight weeks doing their due diligence on the dentistry market. Their investigations strengthened their conviction that they had identified an opportunity that could change the industry. They went back to the VC partner, pitched him, and he went for it. He pitched his partners, and a new "rubber-stamp" partners meeting was scheduled. But things did not go well at that meeting. As the conversation evolved and the tough questions tumbled forward, Eric and Micah were horrified when, hearing the negative tone of his partners, their own sponsor seemed to turn on them in the middle of the meeting. In the end, the firm passed on the deal.

Why? "There were clearly internal politics involved," Eric noted. "But in the end, they hated the idea of investing in dentistry. It's as simple as that." Thus, Eric had found a VC whose investment "sweet spot" did not migrate as he and Micah morphed and shaped their business plan.

Meanwhile, I had been in touch with Eric off and on during this whole process. Like a smart entrepreneur, he kept me informed enough to hook me back into a process, hoping to hedge his bets. Finally, he called me with some big news. "I have good news and bad news," he said over the phone. "The good news is: I've found a promising market. The bad news is: you're going to hate it." In his usual dramatic fashion, he insisted on coming in to talk about the new plan centered on dentistry and promised he'd never bother me again if I didn't like it.

I found myself getting more involved in the Paley movie. It was developing in an interesting way. I liked the new idea enough to do some light diligence. The initial feedback was very positive. If Eric and Micah and team could build a device that scanned the mouth with very high accuracy, it could be a game changer. That realization led to my embarking on heavy due diligence and, eventually, a deal. I met with Eric no fewer than fifteen times over the course of twelve months before finally investing in the company, Brontes 3D. I was impressed with his dogged progress and the achievement of milestones that he had laid out in each of our previous meetings. After getting the company launched and making progress with the technology, Eric began to expose a few of the major industry players to his progress (i.e., to see the movie as well) and track his achievements over the course of a year. That undoubtedly made it easier for him to sell the company successfully to 3M for nearly $100 million—before he had even shipped the first version of the product and with less than $10 million of investment capital.

A scenario like this—where the VC and entrepreneur get to know each other over time and learn each other's preferences, biases, and perspectives—is so much more compelling than a one-hour pitch or thirty-minute conference call. As Polaris Ventures' co-founder and managing partner Terry McGuire (and Sirtris investor) described to me, "The entrepreneur-VC relationship breaks down when people view the partnership as transactional. There is something wonderful about the due diligence courtship. It works best when people take their time to truly understand what they're getting into."

Not all entrepreneurs who are pitching their brains out may feel that way. I'm not sure Gail Goodman of Constant Contact felt particularly "wonderful" getting a hundred rejections while staring at the prospect of not being able to make her next payroll, but with some distance even she would agree with Terry McGuire's general point. Entrepreneurs who can establish the foundation for a productive partnership during the due diligence process will come out better positioned for success on the other side of the market.

A Set of Discrete Experiments with Clear Milestones

One way to think about start-ups like Brontes and Sirtris is as giant experiments. In such cases, VCs much prefer to invest in experiments that are (1) specific and discrete; (2) have very clear assumptions; (3) are not too costly; and (4) have outcomes that can be easily measured over a reasonably short period of time.

Our work with cancer researcher and inventor Dr. Marsha Moses is a good example. A protégé of the late Dr. Judah Folkman, one of the greatest cancer researchers in medical

Marsha Moses

history, and MIT's Bob Langer (profiled in Chapter 1), Dr. Moses had invented a technique to diagnose cancer through biomarkers in urine, which potentially could revolutionize the manner in which cancer is detected and be substantially more cost-effective. In other words, pee in a cup, and Marsha can tell if you have cancer. Making expensive and invasive tests obsolete would enable early detection and potentially save millions of lives.

Marsha's work was the culmination of many years of research. Some of her original discoveries were made in 1995. Once she discovered that these biomarkers could be identified, she started thinking about where that basic discovery might lead. "I started reading about diagnostics on the side—it was my bedtime reading. I was just curious. And I learned that there was a lot of room for improvement."

Marsha's bedtime reading began to blossom into the idea that her research in biomarkers could lead to a diagnostic breakthrough that would transform cancer detection. She began to run side experiments, unfunded, with the help of her lab staff. "No one will believe us," she remembered thinking. "Even though I warned them not to, my team would each check their own urine. Thank goodness no one discovered they had cancer—we probably would have been jailed!"

But to take the promising early experiments out of her lab, bring a product to market, and build a cash-flow-positive company would require a large investment—perhaps $40 million to $50 million. And Marsha clearly didn't view herself as the type of person who would be able to raise that amount. But she wanted her research to somehow find its way to the market. "I am a scientist. I don't think of myself as an entrepreneur," she admitted to me. "But I wanted to make the lives of people with cancer, and the lives of their families, better. By detecting cancer earlier and more effectively, I felt we could increase therapeutic efficacy and survival."

As her research was progressing, a friend of mine happened to visit her lab at Children's Hospital and called me that evening. "Jeff, I don't know anything about this field," my friend confessed, "but if she can really pull this off, it could be very, very valuable." I decided it was worth a look, and my partner who leads our life sciences investments, Michael Greeley, went to visit the lab to see for himself.

After a few meetings, Michael grew very interested, but there were many uncertainties involved. We couldn't yet see the path from lab to commercial launch and exactly how and when the money would be spent. We also knew there would be many risks and value-creating points along the way, including the need to build a management team to partner with the scientists to commercialize the technology and bring it to market. So we decided to work with Marsha and her co-founder, Bruce Zetter, to define a number of key milestones in the process. We agreed to provide only enough capital to fund one step at a time. If the team completed it successfully, with our active help, we'd fund the next one. If not, we'd have a conversation and together decide what to do.

Our first step would be to successfully negotiate the intellectual property out of the hospital. Next, we built a professional commercialization management team, which identified the optimal target market and thought through the ecosystem required to successfully penetrate that market. Finally, we developed a product against that target market and hired a sales force trained to go to market. All of these steps were outlined at the onset in a business plan, with the relevant costs and timelines associated. Each milestone required a different amount of financing, and we pre-negotiated a price for the first few financings based on the value created when each milestone was achieved, followed by an assessment of what the outcomes of the next phase might be.

I asked Marsha about her experience pitching VCs, and her answer surprised me. "It was refreshing," she replied. "It was all very clean. I could simply say, 'This is what we've got. This is how it works.' Monosyllabic answers to questions, of course, but it was straightforward."

Compared to many company founders, Marsha was in a

fortunate position. The science was so good and the idea was so big that my partner Michael was willing to work closely with her to help conceive of the company and bring it out of her lab. But she improved her odds by painting a big vision, explaining it in a clear, straightforward fashion, and then having the deep science to back it up, with well-articulated milestones.

The company that emerged from this collaboration is called Predictive BioSciences, and it is going strong, having now raised over $50 million and making great progress in commercializing the biomarker diagnostics for cancer that were a part of Dr. Moses' original lab work. The story is still evolving, and it's far too early to declare the company a commercial or investment success, but at least the process of taking a scientist and her breakthrough lab work and creating a whole company around it has been very successful.

THE NEXT STEP

Without question, the odds are stacked against the entrepreneur. It can seem hard to get access to a member of the VC club and convince its members that your story is a compelling one and that you have the right team to execute against it. But with good preparation and thoughtful planning, a warm introduction, and a set of well-defined experiments and milestones, you can improve your odds considerably.

And then the natural question arises: Once you secure a VC's interest—then what? How do you actually select the right VC firm and strike a deal? How do you determine the right match?

4

WHEN THE DOG CATCHES THE BUS: MAKING THE PICK AND DOING THE DEAL

What happens when the entrepreneur—like the dog who chases a bus and finally catches it—gets the call from the VC saying, "We're interested"? Does the entrepreneur slam into the side of the bus, like the poor dog Sophie slamming into Fred Wilson's conference room window? Does she get run over? Or does she jump immediately on board?

None of the above, if she is wise.

If the entrepreneur wants to do it right, she enters into a careful, time-consuming process to consummate the relationship that involves deciding whom to go with, making the pick, and hammering out the specific terms of engagement—doing the deal.

CHECK THE TANGIBLES

Making the pick may mean choosing among suitors—assuming, that is, that the entrepreneur has the privilege of choice. Even if only one VC has expressed interest, however, it is still necessary for the entrepreneur to consider her options. If the match between entrepreneur and VC isn't right, it may make more sense to turn down the offer and pursue other financing routes. Hard to do, but necessary. "If I were an entrepreneur given the choice between banging my head against a cinder-block wall for a year or taking money from [unnamed partner from unnamed firm who is known to be extremely difficult to work with]," observes one VC friend of mine, "I'd opt for the wall." Mark Pincus of Zynga relates to the importance of getting the match right. "I think the whole process of getting an investor and management team is a dating process," he told me. "The more that you're really up front and transparent about your likes and dislikes, all of your foibles and warts and theirs, the more likely you are to get the right fit."

The most obvious aspects of the match are the characteristics of the VC firm that are described in Chapter 2. Does the VC firm know anything about your industry? What is their geographical presence and strategy? What stage do they specialize in? How big is their fund? Where are they in the life cycle of the fund? Will they be willing to continue to support the company in a follow-on round and, if so, what are their criteria?

Within a large or complex industry, like biotech or social media, you want to drill down even deeper into the firm's knowledge. As Trinity's Patricia Nakache told me, "Entrepreneurs need to look for domain expertise. 'Does this person know something about my business or technology area? Can they be helpful to me?' The VC should be able to say, 'Look. Here's a bunch of companies that we worked with that have a similar business model to what you're doing.' "

The entrepreneur should select a VC firm with a process not unlike that of hiring an employee or choosing a lawyer or accountant. In fact, entrepreneurs should think of VCs as service providers. Sure, they're giving you money. But in exchange for the equity you "pay" for that cash, you also expect a certain set of services. To ensure you will get the value you are paying for, always check references, even with big name-brand VC firms, and even with individual venture capitalists with well-known track records. Patricia told me, "I have had the experience of entrepreneurs saying to me, 'I don't need to check the references of this venture capitalist, just because of the brand name of the firm.' That's a mistake for entrepreneurs. They should absolutely check references on the individual VC the firm has assigned. You know, some people might be really successful, but they might also be a huge pain to work with."

The best way to check references of a VC firm or an individual venture capitalist is to talk to entrepreneurs the firm has funded and worked with. "We can tell entrepreneurs how great we are till the cows come home," Patricia said. "But the entrepreneur needs to hear it from the CEOs we work with."

Checking the references of prospective VCs is much like reference checking prospective executive hires—you need to not only check the ones they give you, but also the ones they don't provide. You do this by leveraging your connections in the community to find people who know them well professionally and personally.

There are some added subtleties when checking a VC's references. Again, always check the reference of the particular partner who would sit on your board, not just the firm overall.

Although a firm may be great, it doesn't necessarily mean every partner is a great fit for you and your start-up. Next, recognize that, by and large, entrepreneurs are hesitant to give bad references to VCs, particularly if they still have them on their board of directors (and hence those VCs still decide their fate and compensation). On the other hand, some entrepreneurs who had a bad experience or were fired by the board may have a personal axe to grind with the VC and therefore may give an overly negative reference. The entrepreneur must therefore seek out additional background and context for each reference they're checking in order to get a more complete picture. This doesn't mean you should shy away from speaking to entrepreneurs who worked with this particular VC in a tough situation (e.g., a shutdown or otherwise unhappy outcome). On the contrary, those dialogues can be the most informative, so long as they are evaluated with the full context in mind.

Not only will you learn a lot by checking references thoroughly, but also the VC will take it as a sign of thoughtfulness and professionalism. "We are always much more inclined to invest in entrepreneurs who spend time looking into us," Fred Wilson told me. "We think that is the right thing for an entrepreneur to do. Due diligence shows well for the entrepreneur."

All the characteristics I discussed in Chapter 3 matter about a VC firm, but many things that seem important—and that VC firms present as valuable—may not matter very much. When you boil down what value a VC will provide you, there are, in essence, four important areas: (1) strategy; (2) recruiting; (3) business development; and (4) future financing. I'll discuss each of these in the following sections.

The Strategist

The best VCs are those who are skilled at serving as strategic counselors. A small company can't afford a strategic planning department or to pay McKinsey or BCG to provide expensive strategic consulting services. But you can look to your VC to perform this role. The VC can become the CEO's strategic thought partner, teasing out the key issues, challenging the major assumptions, and generally pushing the CEO to step back from the day-to-day tactical, operational activities and focus on the true value-creating decisions that need to be made.

Union Square's Fred Wilson says he likes to think of himself as the entrepreneur's consigliere, but a consigliere with great pattern recognition. "I want to be the person they call when they need some advice. Whether it's 'I've got a problem with sales' or 'We need to raise some more money. What do you think the right way is to go about doing that?' Or, 'I have this big deal. I'm nervous about it because I'm not sure we can actually meet the expectations. But I want the revenue. What do I do?' Those are all big questions. The beauty of being a venture capitalist is we've seen all these issues a lot of times. I've been doing this business for a long time now and I've observed enough to know what's happening and interpret it appropriately."

Twitter's Jack Dorsey says that he did, in fact, think of Fred as his strategic counselor. "Fred had our phone on priority dial, so he could reach us at any time and we could change things instantly. He is very engaged and whenever we need something, we call him up. He is excited to do anything for us." Jack points out that Fred isn't just focused on big-picture strategy, but also on the nitty-gritty features of Twitter as an avid user. "We listen to what he thinks and what he needs from the product," says Jack. "And that has been a great way to get into the relationship and for both of us to trust each other more. As we worked on the product together, we began to learn, 'Oh, this is how Fred is, and this is how Jack is.' We began to learn each other's faults. And that couldn't really happen any other way."

The VC is always trying to give sound strategic advice, but the entrepreneur is not obligated to follow it. The strongest entrepreneurs are the ones who can listen to all the advice from their strategic counselors and then make their own decisions about the right course to follow. "The biggest challenge for a young entrepreneur," Gail Goodman told me, "is having the skill to listen and be open to what the VC is saying, but know when they're wrong, and have the conviction to say when they're wrong. Some of them are giving you really good feedback about things you want to think about. And some of them are just blowing smoke. You don't want to be so arrogant that you don't listen at all. But you don't want to be so susceptible that you're slithering around. You need to have the strength of conviction of your own value."

Just as they wouldn't blindly follow every single recommendation from a McKinsey consultant, the best entrepreneurs need to have that filtering skill to take the good strategy advice from the VCs and chart their own course forward. Keeping your VC in the loop on what you decide is critical, as most VCs I know identify the best CEOs as the ones that bring them in to get their advice on major decisions rather than struggle to keep them out. But the best entrepreneurs know how to make, and take responsibility for, the final call.

The Recruiter

"Admit it, you VCs are really just glorified recruiters," jabbed one of my recruiter friends to me the other day. It made me pause, because the comment rang true. At the time, all eight of my portfolio companies were in the middle of recruiting senior executives to add to their teams. I and the other VC co-investors were knee-deep in trying to help out: participating in weekly recruiting calls, screening candidates, pumping our networks for leads, and partnering in all the activities involved in identifying and filling candidates for the top jobs. This is a common phenomenon throughout our portfolio. Whether it's sourcing great candidates from their network or helping sell a prospective executive on the opportunity at hand, VCs are expected to be a major, positive force in the team-building process on behalf of their companies.

So why is recruiting such a fundamental part of the VC value-added equation? One word: execution. There are a lot of people with good ideas out there trying to start businesses, but very few execute them successfully. Those that can are typically led by an outstanding team that many investors would back in almost any situation. A good team doesn't make a company 10 percent better than a mediocre team; it makes it 1,000 percent better (at roughly the same cost).

In fact, the "VC as recruiter" phenomenon is one of the key reasons many start-ups have become successful. Would Netscape have been nearly as valuable and successful a company without CEO Jim Barksdale, a former Federal Express executive? Where would Google be without Eric Schmidt, the former CEO of Novell who joined the company in the very early days and has led it through its successful IPO and world domination strategy? If a less well-known VC gave Google founders Larry Page and Sergei Brin money rather than John Doerr of Kleiner Perkins, would they have been able to convince Silicon Valley veteran Schmidt to join these two Stanford PhDs and take the CEO gig at Google—never mind have known that he would be the perfect fit there?

Don't bet on it.

Yes, in some ways, the VC *is* a glorified recruiter. However, it would be a mistake to think what recruiting a VC firm can do is equivalent to what an entrepreneur would get from a professional executive search firm. A VC is more focused on the mix of talents needed to improve the start-ups, chances for success and anticipating the right kind of executive that is needed at the right point in the company's life cycle. As Twitter's Jack Dorsey put it, "I would hate to have a VC investor to whom I just send an email to say, 'I need a business development person. Can you make some introductions?' I want a VC who is always thinking a few steps ahead of me. The type of VC who would say, 'Well, I think we're doing this, and therefore we might consider defining this new position in this way and therefore talking to this person.'"

The Business Developer

Some of the most important business relationships for a young start-up are those that a VC might bring to the table.

It is very helpful when the VC's previous investment activities have caused them to build relationships with relevant large and small companies that can help a young start-up get off the ground. Introductions to flagship customers, technology partners, channel partners, and, eventually, potential strategic acquirers often come from VC investors.

VCs can often act as valuable salespeople, rainmakers who can help bring in the "make the company" deal alongside the management team. John Doerr of Kleiner Perkins was a great role model for me at Upromise. We wanted to connect with the CEOs of major consumer companies to convince them of the value of our service. John would take our requests—we would tee him up with an email script and a list of CEOs. He or his assistant (I never knew which) would then march down the list of CEOs and send them the scripted email with the call to action to set up a meeting with my partner, Michael Bronner, or me. With John's help and that of the other investors and advisers around the table, we were able to get in front of nearly every CEO we wanted to meet.

I'm on a board with a VC who asks our CEO to include in every board presentation the five top introductions to prospective partners and customers he'd like us to make for him. VCs often compete with each other based on the quality of their Rolodex. "Who knows the chief marketing officer at Pepsi?" one of my portfolio CEOs asked the board the other day. I raised my hand like an eager kid in the classroom, dutifully took down the action item to reach out to this particular executive, and followed up assiduously to help foster a connection. Every VC aspires to be that go-to resource. By actively trolling around the halls of Microsoft, Google, IBM, Apple, EMC,

P&G, and other behemoths, VCs build executive relationships that can help provide connections to their little portfolio companies that aspire to do business with these giants. If your VC isn't serving as one of your best executive-level door openers, you have chosen the wrong VC.

The Financier

Whenever an entrepreneur has secured VC money in a first round of financing, there is almost always a second round. Rare is the company that is able to develop a strong, sustainable cash-flow-positive business with a single round of financing. Over the course of a ten-year entrepreneurial career, a start-up CEO might seek four or five rounds of financing. An active VC is usually involved in four or five rounds of financing each year as well—typically two new ones and two or three follow-on investments in their portfolio. Thus, the VC can be a helpful coach during the follow-on fund-raising process. The most obvious thing a VC can do is to write another check from his fund. The less obvious ones are to make introductions to other potential investors and serve as a coach during the due diligence and negotiation process. VCs have been on the receiving end of pitch after pitch and, therefore, once they are on your side, they can be a great resource for determining the best way to position your company to the market.

"The real value-add from a VC comes down to future financing," Reid Hoffman told me. "The principal thing that a firm can bring you is ease in the next round of financing." In some cases, it is because of the quality of the brand. For example, take Sequoia Capital, one of the best-known and best-regarded VCs in the world and the backer of Cisco, Google, Yahoo!, and YouTube—and of Reid Hoffman's companies, LinkedIn and PayPal. When they invest in a company, it is labeled "a Sequoia deal," and Sequoia-backed CEOs take great pride in the association. When another VC learns that Sequoia has invested in a company, it adds immediate panache to that company. Sequoia-backed companies are thus able to raise money from other VCs more easily than your average VC-backed company.

When the entrepreneur is ready for follow-on financing, one particularly tricky area to navigate for the VC and the entrepreneur is whether the follow-on round should be an "inside round," where the current investors make the full investment without any outside participation, or an "outside round," which is led by an outside investor and some or all of the existing investors participate alongside the new lead investor. On the one hand, an inside round saves everyone (especially the management team) time and hassle—no need to go outside and pitch twenty or thirty VCs on what you're doing and overcome all their objections to raise money. On the other hand, by attracting a new investor, an outside round brings another deep pocket to the table. Further, if the entrepreneur and existing VCs disagree about the appropriate price for the next round of financing, an outside investor provides an objective perspective on the appropriate price for the next round.

I call this the "inside-out, outside-in" dance, and it was always a mystery to me when I was an entrepreneur. If the VCs around the table love the company, why would they want anyone else to invest in it and dilute their ownership? Why not keep investing and continue to (one of my favorite VC aphorisms) "put more money to work"? (Whenever I hear this VC phrase, I imagine a bunch of George Washington dollar bills hunched over their PCs typing out code while a VC foreman barks at them: "More! I need to get more dollars to work!") This dance can have several variations.

Is it that the VCs only push their entrepreneurs to raise money from outsiders in situations where they don't love the company and otherwise would want to hoard the investment opportunity? But if all VCs behaved this way, then all VCs would know this. Therefore, when a VC receives "the call" from a VC buddy (sotto voce: "I'm only exposing this to a few folks, it's moving fast, but I wanted to get you introduced to it because you have such unique value-add and we have such a unique relationship"), the savvy VC buddy gets very suspicious. My partner, David Aronoff, refers to this as the "VC buddy pass," and warned me when I got into the business to run for the hills when it comes your way.

And then there's the famous bait and switch technique—the VC board member loves the company, but the other partners in the firm are more skeptical and insist on seeking outside validation. So, the VC pushes management to spend countless hours running a financing process to attract interest from new investors. However, once the outside term sheet is secured, the insiders decide that they actually do want to invest in the company and keep the round to themselves and shut out (and annoy) the outsider. This is known as the "rock fetch." VC to entrepreneur: "Go find me a rock." Entrepreneur returns, panting hard with a rock in hand. VC examines the rock, tosses it to the side, and sniffs, "No, I don't like that rock, go fetch me another one."

All kidding aside, there are often genuinely good reasons for high-quality start-up companies to seek outside-led rounds.

The financing capacity of the existing investors certainly plays into the equation. And, despite my above cynical remarks, true value-add and market validation can be very important to both the entrepreneur and the VC.

How can an entrepreneur avoid these land mines while trying to successfully conduct the outside-in, inside-out dance? First, be proactive and have a frank discussion with your VCs about the next round the day after you close the first round. Something like: "If I hit these milestones, will you continue to support the company? If so, what is the price increase that we will deserve? What if we exceed the milestones by 20 percent? What if we miss the milestones by 20 percent?" Also, it's perfectly normal and appropriate to have some tension around price. The entrepreneur is always going to think her start-up is worth more than the VC. Therefore, it may make sense for the entrepreneur to go outside to validate what is a fair, market-based price and terms. Besides, cultivating additional VC relationships for future rounds of financing can often be a good time investment for the entrepreneur.

Ultimately, the outside-in, inside-out dance can waste a lot of time and create unnecessary tension between the VC and the entrepreneur. But, like most things, if the communication is open and direct, the dance can end very well for all parties when the music stops.

LOOK FOR CHEMISTRY

So now you have a sense of the role that VCs can and should play in the start-up. With that framework in mind, let's turn to the entrepreneur's process for revealing the pros and cons of working with different VCs and their different firms. For me, and for all the VCs and entrepreneurs I spoke with for this book, the most essential element in the relationship between the entrepreneur and the VC boils down to one word.

Chemistry.

When I say chemistry, however, I'm not talking about friendship or social compatibility or finding a drinking buddy. Yes, being socially compatible is a plus for entrepreneurs and VCs. You often hear the refrain, "Life's too short to invest in people you don't like." But the real emphasis on chemistry concerns the thinking styles, ways of working, enthusiasm for the business, and a shared view of the future. You want to find someone you think you can work with and someone you believe you can trust.

Tim Bucher has learned the importance of chemistry in spades over the years. Tim is one of Silicon Valley's most accomplished serial entrepreneurs. A former Sun engineer, co-founder of WebTV (sold to Microsoft), a former Apple executive (ran all of Macintosh engineering), and founder of Zing Systems (sold to Dell), Tim may be the only entrepreneur on the planet who has worked closely with Scott McNealy, Michael Dell, Bill Gates, *and* Steve Jobs. My partner Jon Karlen led an investment in Tim's Zing Systems, which developed a mobile music software platform to compete with the iPhone, and we had the pleasure of working closely with him and learning some of the secrets to his repeated entrepreneurial success.

Having worked with numerous VCs, good and bad, Tim points to chemistry as a key success factor. "The chemistry piece is so critical with the VC partners you team up with," he

Tim Bucher

told me. "If you're doing a pitch and everyone is all stodgy but they want to do an investment, even if they give you the best term sheet and everything, stay away from that. I'd rather take the lower offer, the lower term sheet, but work with folks that can become part of the team."

Picking a VC who can operate as a part of the team is a theme Tim emphasized over and over again in our conversation, as did the other entrepreneurs with whom I spoke. Being an entrepreneur is a lonely and stressful job. A good VC helps make it less lonely, providing an open ear and strong support.

Reid Hoffman of LinkedIn agrees. "In the end, I pick the individual that I most want to work with," Reid explained to me. "It's a critical hiring decision. It's maybe not quite as critical as hiring a CEO, but it's damn important."

The definition of the best individual venture capitalist to work with will be different for every entrepreneur. Jack Dorsey, Mr. Twitter, was looking for a VC who had passion for his market, could help him with his product, and could challenge his thinking. Jack talked with many VCs when he was trying to get financing for Twitter, starting with firms on the West Coast. "We had a lot of conversations with people down in the Valley," Jack said. "At the end of the pitch, the person across the table would say, 'Well, we'll let you know fairly soon, like in an hour or so. We just want to talk internally, but we're really excited.' We didn't react well to that. We wanted to be questioned, we wanted to be challenged, and we wanted to see some of their thinking around actually developing this product."

For whatever reason, Jack found more of those challenging VCs on the East Coast than on the West Coast. "I think it was just an attitude thing," he said. "I found the East Coast to be a little bit more aggressive. They say what they mean in the hopes of just moving on right away. On the West Coast, people were a little bit more laid back. If they thought we were going down the wrong path, they wouldn't necessarily say it, but they might make it known in an indirect way. I just didn't appreciate that at all."

Jack ended up with NYC-based Fred Wilson at Union Square Ventures. "We turned down a bunch of VCs," Jack said. "We saw a name, but there wasn't enough behind the name immediately. A VC has to show me right away that I can trust them. It's hard to do. But when it's right, it's right. And we were very fortunate in it being right with Fred. He was very aggressive, in a good way, in a thinking way. He had no subtlety at all. But more importantly, he was a day-to-day user of our service and he obviously loved it. He came to the pitch with a bunch of requests for features and lots of questions about why we had done what we had done. That helped clarify our thinking around the product and it helped clarify our thinking around the company. And that's exactly what we wanted in the boardroom."

During their courting period, Fred showed Jack he could provide more than just money; he could contribute to the product's vision and direction to help lead the company to success. If your VC doesn't show you that passion for your product and your own personal success, as well as an ability to add value during the due diligence process through their strategic or product insight, then he and his firm may not be the right business partner for you.

DO THE DEAL

Of course, it's not *only* about chemistry.

Once you find the right VC for your company and both sides conclude it makes sense to move forward, you need to negotiate the deal—setting out the key business terms of the investment and the legal framework in which you're going to operate. This negotiation can be the first real test of how well the entrepreneur and the venture capitalist are going to work together. One of my favorite sayings at our firm is, "You learn a lot about entrepreneurs when you're in the crucible of a deal with them." Do they respond defensively to the really sensitive due diligence questions, such as discussing past failures or prior unproductive business relationships? Do they appear to be on top of the details of the business model? Do they seem hesitant to turn over customer and management references to you and provide full transparency? On the other hand, if they are smart, prompt, organized, and open, you can assume this is an indicator of how they'll handle themselves after the honeymoon period of selling you on their company is over.

And, perhaps most important, do they seem honest and straight, delivering bad news as well as good news throughout the process? For example, I had one situation where a CEO revealed to me that his technical co-founder was moving to Spain for personal reasons right in the final stages of the funding process. He was nervous about telling me but did it in an honest and open way as soon as he found out. His candor was compelling to me, and his plan for recovery was pragmatic and thoughtful, so we still funded the company.

On the flip side, an entrepreneur can learn a lot about VCs during the due diligence process. Are they clear in communicating the key due diligence issues transparently through the process? Do they show up on time for meetings? Do they appear prepared and focused or disorganized and distracted? Do they follow through on their commitments, especially their investment decision-making process and timeline? Whatever traits an entrepreneur observes in the prospective VC during the honeymoon period of due diligence will come out again in spades during the duration of their relationship. One VC friend of mine likes to tell entrepreneurs that if he doesn't add value in some way during the due diligence process—either through valuable introductions, good strategic advice, or simply helping sharpen their fund-raising pitch—he tells them they shouldn't do business with him.

CONTRACT: THE TERM SHEET

To understand the typical deal, we need to analyze the "term sheet" and examine some of its key elements.

The term sheet is essentially a preliminary, nonbinding document between the entrepreneur and the VC that outlines the material provisions of the financing deal. Some VCs issue a term sheet early in the process to lock up the deal—and keep the entrepreneur from going elsewhere—while they decide whether they really want to invest. Entrepreneurs need to be wary of these situations and not be afraid to push the VC to define more clearly whether the term sheet represents a real commitment or merely a discussion document. The specter of "pulling the term sheet"—or rescinding on the offer to invest, perhaps if the VC did not properly get her partnership aligned behind the decision—arises in situations where the VC and entrepreneur haven't been clear with each other on expectations and ground rules.

Most VCs issue a term sheet to the entrepreneur only when they have made a final decision—the entire partnership has decided and business-related due diligence is complete. There may still be "legal" due diligence, such as when it becomes necessary to confirm that the company's charter and incorporation papers were done properly or to verify the intellectual property. In the case where the term sheet is duly issued, the financing closes and the money is wired, typically within thirty to forty-five days from signing the term sheet.

Another version of bad behavior on the part of VCs is the "exploding term sheet"—here's our term sheet but only if you decide to accept it within twenty-four hours. This should be a red flag for the entrepreneur. The VC-entrepreneur relationship is one that needs to be entered into with great thought and deliberation. Neither side should pressure the other to rush in.

Different VCs like to include different levels of detail in their term sheets. Some term sheets are two or three pages long and at a very high level, with only a handful of provisions, under the assumption that the "definitive documents" (i.e., the detailed closing contract that spells out the particulars of the financing) will cover the finer details. Others are very detailed, with twenty or thirty provisions laying out all the important economic and legal elements of a deal such that the definitive document requires little additional negotiation. A good lawyer with experience negotiating VC transactions is a necessity to assist the entrepreneur in navigating this complicated process, but it is the entrepreneur who must lead the way and understand the various implications of her decisions.[11]

In essence, there are two issues that really matter to the VC in a financing transaction: economics and control.[12] The economics is more than just the price the investor pays for the equity. Yes, price matters. But price in VC deals tends not to be as simple as one might think. There are important terms and conditions that impact the price and the manner in which the economic pie is split between the investor and the entrepreneur. Control refers to the mechanisms that allow investors to exert their decision-making authority and will on the company.

Let's analyze the economics first.

Economics (Not Only "Price")

The discussion of price centers around the pre-money valuation—what is the company worth prior to the VC's investment? This pre-money valuation is known in shorthand

---

11. A great resource for entrepreneurs is the term sheet and definitive agreement templates and model documents that the National Venture Capital Association publishes at www.nvca.org.

12. Many thanks and acknowledgment to fellow VC and prolific blogger Brad Feld of Foundry Group and his partner, Jason Mendelson, for their sage counsel and excellent posts on this topic, which can be found in the archives of Brad's blog at www.feld.com/blog/archives/term_sheet.

as "the pre-money" or just "the pre," and you will hear entrepreneurs and VCs discussing other company finances using
this term. ("You were able to raise money at a ten-million-
dollar pre? Life isn't fair. I had to struggle to get to a four-
million pre and I have a prototype and real customers!")

Determining the pre-money valuation is an art, not a science, and many entrepreneurs get frustrated with what seems
like an opaque process. Unlike what you learn in a finance class
in business school, where you calculate discounted cash flows
and apply a weighted average cost of capital, there is no magic
formula. The valuation for entrepreneurial ventures is set in
a back-and-forth negotiation based on three factors: (1) the
amount of capital that the entrepreneur is trying to raise in
order to prove out the first set of milestones; (2) the VC's target ownership (often 20-30 percent); (3) how competitive the
deal is (that is, if the entrepreneur has numerous VCs chasing
them, they can drive up the price).

I've seen pre-money valuations range from a typical $3-$6
million all the way up to $80 million, which is what our
pre-money valuation was in our first round of financing at
Upromise. That was an unusual time in history, the late 1990s
and early 2000, where companies with only a few million dollars in revenue were going public for billion-dollar valuations.
In most situations today, the initial pre-money valuation is
under $10 million. In the end, the VC has to be convinced that
he can make five to ten times his money in three to five years
and so backs into the valuation with that heuristic in mind.

But the pre-money isn't the only term that defines price:
The post-money plays a part as well. The post-money is the
pre-money plus the money raised. That is, if a company raises

$4 million at a pre-money valuation of $6 million, then the post-money is $10 million. Thus, the investors who provided the $4 million own 40 percent of the company and the management team (founders, employees, executives) owns 60 percent.

Another term that impacts the price is the size of the option pool. Most VCs invest in companies that need to hire additional management team members, sales and marketing personnel, and technical talent to build the business. Some start-ups begin life with a founding team that aspires to hire a strong outside executive as CEO. These new hires typically receive stock options, and the issuance of those stock options dilutes the other shareholders.

In anticipation of those hiring needs, many VCs will require that an option pool with unallocated stock options be created, thereby forming a stock option budget for new hires that will be set aside to avoid further dilution. The stock option pool typically comes out of the management team allocation (i.e., the option pool is included in the pre-money valuation), independent of the VC investment ownership. In the example above of $4 million invested in a $6 million pre-money valuation (known in VC-speak shorthand as "4 on 6"), if the VCs insist on an unallocated stock option pool of 20 percent, then the VC investors still own 40 percent and the remaining 60 percent is split between a 20 percent unallocated stock option pool at the discretion of the board and a 40 percent stake owned by the management team. In other words, the existing management team/founders have given up 20 percentage points of their 60 percent ownership in order to reserve it for future management hires.

This relationship between option pool size and price isn't

always understood by entrepreneurs, but is well understood by VCs. I learned it the hard way in the first term sheet that I put forward to an entrepreneur. I was competing with another firm. We put forward a "6 on 7" deal with a 20 percent option pool. In other words, we would invest (alongside another VC) $6 million at a $7 million pre-money valuation to own 46 percent of the company (6 divided by 6+7). The founders would own 34 percent and would set aside a stock option pool of 20 percent for future hires. One of my competitors put forward a "6 on 9" deal, in other words, $6 million invested at a $9 million pre-money valuation to own 40 percent of the company (6 divided by 6+9). But my competitor inserted a larger option pool than I did—30 percent—so the founders would only receive 30 percent of the company as compared to my offer that gave them 34 percent. The entrepreneur chose the competing deal. When I asked why, he looked me in the eye and said, "Jeff—their price was better. My company is worth more than seven million."

At the time, I wasn't facile enough with the nuances to argue against his faulty logic. But later, we instituted a policy at Flybridge to talk about the "promote" for the founding team rather than just the "pre." The "promote," as we have called it, is the founding team's ownership percentage multiplied by the post-money valuation.

Back to my example of the "6 on 7" deal with the 20 percent option pool. The founding team owns 34 percent of a company with a $13 million post-money valuation. In other words, they have a $4.4 million "promote" (13 x 0.34) in exchange for their founding contributions. Note that in the "6 on 9" deal, the founding team had a nearly identical promote: 30 percent of a $15 million post-money valuation, or $4.5 million. In other words, my offer was basically identical to the competing offer; it just had a lower pre-money valuation and a smaller option pool.

Note that this pricing framework assumes that the financing is the first money that has been invested in the company (i.e., it is the Series A round of financing). If there is already invested capital in the company (i.e., someone has already invested in a Series A and the entrepreneur is now raising a Series B round of financing), then the Series A investors have two competing motivations. Assuming they want to put more money into the company, they will either seek to raise capital at the highest price possible from outside investors in order to limit dilution on their earlier money (and limit the amount of new capital they put in at the higher price) or invest their own capital at a price lower than (down round) or equal to (flat round) the previous round. It all depends on how bullish they are about the company's future and how much money they have invested in the company already as compared to their target figure as a function of their overall fund size.

Another nuanced element of the economic equation of a term sheet is the liquidation preference. The liquidation preference is the governing formula for how the proceeds from a liquidity event are divided (i.e., who gets preference over whom when dividing the pie). The two pieces of the liquidation preference formula are (1) the preference calculation and (2) participation. The preference calculation is typically straight-forward—those who have invested capital get preference in any liquidation over other claim holders, e.g., common stock-holders who haven't invested capital, but have a stake in the company through their ownership of common stock. In some cases, preferred stockholders seek more than simply 1x their invested capital (where "x" is the amount of capital invested) and demand a 2x or 3x liquidation preference. That is, if an investor invests $5 million in a company and the company sells for $10 million, the investor gets all $10 million in the case of a 2x liquidation preference and other stockholders (i.e., common stock owners) get nothing. Under normal market conditions, multiple liquidation preferences are rare in the early stage or very competitive deals, but quite common in recapitalizations or distressed situations.

The participation feature of the preferred shares is the other part of the preference equation that the entrepreneur needs to factor in when evaluating the economics of the deal. Preferred stock participation governs what happens to the remaining proceeds after the initial preference is paid out to the investors. There are three general flavors of participation: fully participating, non-participating, and (in between) capped participation.

Fully participating preferred stock means that the preferred shareholders will share in the liquidation proceeds, after the payment of the liquidation preference, on a pro rata basis as if they had converted their preferred shares into common stock. For example, let's assume the preferred shareholders own 60 percent of the company for a $5 million investment and they have a 1x liquidation preference that is participating. If the company sells for $15 million, then the first investors get their liquidation preference ($5 million) and also get to participate in their 60 percent share of the remaining $10 million of the proceeds, or $6 million, for a total of $11 million in return to the investors.

If the preferred shares were not participating in the above example, then the investors would choose to either take their $5 million preference back or convert their preferred stock to common stock and take their pro rata share of the total proceeds, which would be 60 percent of $15 million, or $9 million—a wise choice. In the case of non-participating preferred shares, the investors are making sure their money comes out first. Once that threshold is cleared, they benefit precisely according to their ownership position. An investor with non-participating preferred shares may be misaligned with the entrepreneur in some circumstances. For example, at Flybridge Capital Partners, we have a portfolio company where we own 10 percent of the company with a total of $5 million invested and our investment is in a non-participating preferred class of shares. If the company were to sell for $5 million, we would get our $5 million back. If the company were to sell for $50 million, we would still only get $5 million back (10 percent of $50 million). In an example like this, a VC may be indifferent between exit outcomes anywhere between $5 million and $50 million. If the entrepreneur owns 30 percent of the business, she is clearly not indifferent within that range. Hence, there is misalignment between the VC and the entrepreneur in terms of incentives related to outcomes.

Making explicit these pockets of misalignment and talking them through openly is often as critical as the particulars of the participation feature in the preferred stock being purchased. One useful technique for clarifying the various scenarios is to have a simple spreadsheet with the entrepreneur-VC split laid out under different exit outcomes. This distribution of proceeds in the event of a sale is often called the "waterfall," evoking an image of sale proceeds cascading like a river to various shareholders, and I recommend entrepreneurs be clear about what the waterfall calculations look like for each of the preferred and common shareholders.

In between the two extremes of fully participating and non-participating is a technique many VCs like to use, which is called capped participation. In capped participation, the VCs set a certain price per share threshold, under which the preferred shares are participating, but over which they are non-participating. The logic behind this provision is simple: VCs aren't in the business of giving entrepreneurs capital to make one or two times their money. Their objective, and the entrepreneur's vision, is that the company will be so successful that investors will make more than ten times their money. If a company doesn't live up to its promise, investors want to get their money out first, if there is a sale, and they want to make a little extra in exchange for their capital being tied up over the years. This scenario is sometimes called the "sideways scenario," and VCs feel as if they deserve a preferred return under this scenario. But if things go well and the company sells for five or ten times the original purchase price, then everyone should simply get their share. In the example above, where the investors own 50 percent for $5 million, a capped participation deal might stipulate that participation stop when the proceeds are three or more times the purchase price. If the proceeds are less than threefold, then the preferred is participating, providing an extra bit of return on capital for the investor. The logic is simple for a VC investor. If a VC investor gives you $5 million for half your company, and after a few years you consume that capital to grow and sell the company for $10 million, then you turned the VC investor's $5 million into, um, $5 million. The VC investor makes nothing, and you make $5 million for yourself. Many VCs complain that this isn't a fair deal.

Many early-stage VCs are advocates for "clean terms," which usually means capped or no participation and few bells and whistles around the edges to maintain alignment. The other reason early-stage VCs argue for clean terms is that they are savvy enough to know that the early-stage terms carry forward in the later stages of a company's life. Later-stage investors are likely to punish early-stage investors disproportionately if the terms are onerous, layering capital on top of the early-stage investors while inheriting all the privileges and preferences that the early-stage investors put in place. Further, if there are too many encumbrances on management, they will be negotiated away in later stages if the entrepreneurs get more leverage as a result of good performance.

Fairness and precedent may have some impact on the negotiations, but the real question is who has the most leverage in the transaction. If the entrepreneur has choices and the VC cares enough to win, they will cave on many of the key terms. The typical line you'll hear within the halls of a VC partnership when pursuing a competitive deal is, "If we like the deal at $8 million pre, and we think it'll be a billion-dollar company, then why wouldn't we invest at a $10 million pre if that's what it takes to win the deal?" On the other hand, if the VC doesn't detect much competitive pressure and if the deal is somewhat controversial within the partnership, he will take a harder line on terms.

Your Price, My Terms: Who's in Control?

Some investors play the game of "your price, my terms" where they accede to an entrepreneur's pre-money demands, but load up the option pool and the liquidation preference in such a way that the economic equation would be more favorable if the entrepreneur took a lower price in exchange for what is known as a "clean deal."

So those are the key elements of the economics—pre-money price, option pool, and participation. Now let's move on to the topic of control.

In most VC term sheets, the framework for who controls what decisions has been carefully thought through. Even the most experienced serial entrepreneurs have at most three or four data points of experience over, say, fifteen years of running start-ups while the VC partnership has over a hundred data points over a similar period of time. Thus, the VC has seen every possible scenario where the control provisions come into play and is careful to manage these "edge cases."

At the summary level, there are three control elements for the entrepreneur to focus on in a term sheet. First is the composition of the board of directors. The board has the power to fire and hire the CEO and decide on major transactions, such as when to sell the company and what follow-on financings should look like. The entrepreneur who doesn't think through the board composition carefully can often find himself on the short end of these decisions.

The composition of the board is often a reflection of the ownership split between the entrepreneur and the VC. Let's take an example of a $4 million on $4 million Series A deal, where two VCs own 25 percent each so that 50 percent is in the hands of the investors, where there is a 20 percent option pool for future hires, and the founders own the remaining 30 percent. The board is likely to be a five-member board. Typically, the smaller the board, the better, as it will be far more efficient in making important decisions. In such cases, the board is typically split as follows: two board seats for the two VC investors; one board seat set aside for the CEO (who may or may not be the founder); one board seat for the common shareholders (i.e., the founders); and one independent board seat, typically an industry expert and/or CEO in a related field whose Rolodex, experience and sage advice can add value to the company.

Do the VCs "control" the board and therefore the company in this example? Well, it depends on the fine print of board composition. If the independent director is unilaterally selected by the VCs, then, yes, they in effect control the board because they have two seats and get to choose the third unilaterally. If the independent director must be mutually agreed to, then the VCs only control the board if the CEO or the independent director is on their side. In practice, the CEO is unlikely to go against the VCs' will if the VCs are the only source of funding (i.e., the company is still not cash-flow-positive and needs additional funding support from their VCs). Further, the VCs are often members of the compensation committee that sets the CEO's salary and bonus. So, in practice, the VCs do control the board in this case and in many cases as a result of the term sheet framework they put in when they invested in the start-up.

The second control element VCs insert in term sheets is the list of protective provisions. These are the provisions that require approval from the VCs, not just the board, to make certain decisions. The list can be long in typical VC term sheets, but the net of it is: You won't make any major decisions (buy any companies, sell your company, make major investments, go into debt) without VC approval. Sometimes the protective provisions are worded such that the veto power is in the hands of the board and at other times it's explicit that the veto power is in the hands of the VCs (e.g., when you see language like "requiring the consent of both Preferred Directors"). Some VCs may feel comfortable with a more independently structured board making some of the major decisions, but the control of other major decisions (e.g., when to sell the company or when to accept a new financing with new terms that change the control elements) is typically held very closely by the investing VC firms. If the VCs can control the board and the board controls the major decisions, well, you get the picture.

A third important control element in the term sheet is the combination of voting threshold and drag-along rights. Voting threshold means that more than a majority vote, or the preferred stock vote, is required for major actions. If the VCs own most of the preferred stock, and the preferred stock vote is required for major transactions, then the VCs exert control through this vehicle. Drag-along rights mean that it doesn't matter how you vote your shares; if the majority or a defined supermajority vote is required for a certain action (a threshold typically set to ensure that the VCs' vote carries the day), then the other shareholders are "dragged along" and must comply with that major action (e.g., selling the company or accepting another round of financing).

All of this may sound a bit Machiavellian, but it's important that entrepreneurs understand how the VCs are looking at things. If everything goes well, most of the control-oriented term sheet provisions never come into play—it's all discussion, earnest debate, and aligned decisions. But when things go poorly and there are disagreements, the VC is often in the driver's seat to make major decisions. Only in very rare circumstances can the entrepreneur retain full control. Typically, VCs negotiate deals and make investments only when they can "control their capital"—a euphemism for controlling major decisions, particularly financial ones, in the companies in which they invest their capital.

The reason many entrepreneurs are paranoid about the control elements in a term sheet is their emotional attachment to their start-up and their fear of getting fired. Mark Pincus, founder and CEO of the wildly successful gaming company Zynga (maker of FarmVille and Mafia Wars, with over 230 million monthly active users playing its games), puts it simply: "All that we feel, as an entrepreneur, is the negative side. 'They want to get control of my company. They want to meddle. They want to second-guess me if things go bad and then, ultimately, fire and replace me.'"

The control elements in the term sheet—and the importance that both VCs and entrepreneurs place on them when the rubber hits the road—make it all the more important that entrepreneurs choose VC partners who they can trust. When a founding team takes in VC money, they are taking on a business partner. Or as Jack Dorsey of Twitter put it to me, "When selecting our VC partner, I knew I was hiring a boss I couldn't fire." When VCs start invoking control provisions in investment documents, it is almost never a happy scenario and usually the root cause is a breakdown in trust between the VC and entrepreneur.

Let me reiterate an important piece of advice: Find a good lawyer, the earlier in the process the better. The key is to find a lawyer who has done enough VC deals that he can explain what the meaning is behind each nook and cranny, while at the same time being strong-minded and independent enough from the VCs that he is not beholden to them. There are many other terms you will see in the term sheet that your lawyer can walk you through and explain, but remember to stay focused on economics and control above all else.

How Much Money Should I Raise?

The final important question in working through the deal with the VC is how much money the entrepreneur should raise. Once they've secured VC interest, there can be a fair amount of flexibility on this point. But there are important trade-offs to consider.

More money provides more runway and room for mistakes, but at the cost of some additional dilution. Twitter's Jack Dorsey recalled a conversation he had with Netscape founder and angel investor Marc Andreessen. "Marc advised us very early on to take as much money as we could, because a recession was coming and everything was going to hit the fan. And this was in early 2008, maybe the end of 2007. And he's like, 'I know you're worried about dilution, but just try to get as much money as you can, build a war chest so you can weather the storm, because the storm is coming.'"

On the other hand, raising less money in a more capital-efficient fashion reduces your dilution while increasing your exit options. If a company raises more capital, the investors are by definition in at a higher price. A company that has raised $5 million on a $10 million pre for a $15 million post-money valuation will typically make their VCs happy if they sell for any price above $75 million, or a fivefold return for the invested capital. But if that same company chooses to raise $15 million on the same $10 million valuation, they now have a post-money valuation of $25 million. The same fivefold multiplier would require a sale of $125 million.

The result is that although the entrepreneur may be thrilled with a $100 million exit opportunity (calculating, say, their 20 percent stake at $20 million), the VC may not be as happy and may try to block the transaction to play for a bigger win. The VC and the entrepreneur can be misaligned here—the VC is swinging for the fences and has many chances in their portfolio to generate enough returns to ensure success for their $500 million fund, while the entrepreneur may feel this is their one shot and being a multimillionaire is good enough. That's the downside of taking in too much money—the more money you raise, the more pressure there is to generate a large return.

Another consideration to weigh in deciding how much money to raise is whether to form an investment syndicate of multiple firms. Many entrepreneurs prefer to have two firms as investors to provide twice the value-add (recruiting, strategy, business development), deeper pockets for future financing rounds, and simply to balance each other out so that no one firm or individual can dominate the board. Others prefer to work with only one firm to keep things simple and streamlined (one decision maker) and to minimize the amount of capital and therefore dilution they will face (multiple firms will, in aggregate, typically prefer to own and invest incrementally more than one firm alone). Some VCs prefer to control the process of choosing the co-investor, and some are open to the entrepreneur driving the process.

When raising money and considering syndication, simply make sure you find out whether the firm is open to syndication or not—many have an explicit policy on such matters—and think through what might be the best approach for your particular situation.

START THINGS OFF RIGHT

In the end, entrepreneurs need to raise the right amount of capital for their business, under terms they can live with (and can achieve under the circumstances) from VCs with whom they have great chemistry and who they believe will be good business partners for the long, hard journey. It's difficult enough to build a large, valuable company from scratch. Imagine if you get some of these key decisions wrong and start off with the wind in your face. But the right decisions and the right VCs put you in a position with the wind at your back, allowing you to focus on all the tough challenges of building a business and creating value in your start-up.

5

AS THE START-UP TURNS:
EVERY COMPANY IS A SOAP OPERA

When I was a kid, my older sisters would come home from school, turn on the TV, and watch soap operas until dinner. I sat on the floor organizing my baseball cards while they gasped their way through *As the World Turns* and *General Hospital*. As a VC, I sometimes feel like the soaps are on again. Start-up companies have plot twists that seem borrowed from *The Young and the Restless* and larger-than-life characters straight out of *Dynasty* or *Mad Men*. Genius entrepreneurs pursuing their impossible dreams against all odds. Shrewd venture capitalists seeking gold and glory. Mad scientists. Wily CEOs. Crafty competitors. Greedy bankers. Tens of millions of dollars at stake. Lives and careers on the line. Unexpectedly, surprises at every turn.

Virtually all entrepreneurs I know have told me they could write a book about the trials and travails of some of their start-ups. They usually think their story is unique, but although no two are exactly the same, they tend to have similar characters, dramatic tensions, and ups and downs in the action. The drama is usually the result of mistakes that entrepreneurs make, often as a result of misunderstanding the behavior pattern of start-ups and VCs. But as Mark Pincus of Zynga put it to me forcefully, "Don't be a victim. It's not the VC's fault. Don't look at [the drama and conflicts] personally, look at them structurally." By learning from the mistakes of other entrepreneurs, you can avoid making their mistakes (and make your own new ones instead!)

FROM THE JUNGLE TO THE HIGHWAY

One of the hardest things about getting a new company off the ground is the challenge of achieving so many fundamental things at the same time. Running an existing business, a manager can focus her energies on a few high-priority items and count on the other things coasting along. In a start-up, nothing coasts along. Everything has to be done, fast, and at the same time.

Think about how hard starting a company from scratch really is. The entrepreneur needs to sell venture capitalists on her vision in order to raise money ("This is going to be huge") and promise them that a killer senior executive team and strategic business partners are lined up to jump on board right after financing. At the same time, the entrepreneur needs to recruit senior executives by promising them adequate financing and powerful partners. Meanwhile, strategic partners need to be secured with the promise of plentiful financing and a strong execution team to follow through on the promises.

There are typically three phases to the start-up company process: (1) the jungle; (2) the dirt road; and (3) the highway.

In the jungle, the entrepreneurs have no set path to follow and must hack at the foliage to get from point A to point B, diving into different parts of the jungle with reckless abandon. No one has been there before them and they simply have to make it up as they go along. There are some casualties along the way, but the determined entrepreneurs change direction, adjust plans, and figure out a way to get out of the jungle. While in this stage of their growth, the entrepreneur's metric for success is how much "buzz" or positive word of mouth they can generate about the company. One of my former bosses liked to joke that at this early stage of development, the company's PR (public relations) ratio was far more important than its PE (price to earnings) ratio.

Once they are out of the jungle, the entrepreneur finds a dirt road. At this stage, they are shipping product, generating revenue, and have a clear sense of strategic direction. Their goal is to begin to increase their momentum along their chosen path. There may be a few twists and turns and plenty of bumps, but it's not nearly as chaotic as things were in the jungle—target customers are established, competitors are well known and understood, and fewer surprises intrude on their progress. At this stage, the success metric for the company is revenue growth. The absolute revenue number matters less than the ongoing growth. The more promotionally minded entrepreneurs will refer to that growth in every conversation possible.

After reaching the end of the dirt road, the entrepreneur discovers the highway. Suddenly, the company is no longer entrepreneurial. You're charging ahead with such a speed that you now have less room or ability to maneuver. You pray you don't slam into a wall (i.e., run out of cash) but instead continue to progress on a smooth path to an IPO and beyond. To succeed in this stage the company needs to be profitable, and so now the entrepreneur cites cash flow figures rather than describing the arc of revenue growth.

Different management teams are better suited for different parts of the process. The entrepreneur who is well suited for hacking through the jungle and avoiding pitfalls may not be the right executive to lead the company when it is firmly rolling down the highway. The people, organization structure, communication processes, and everything else that make up a business thus all evolve rapidly during these phases. For high-growth businesses, that can mean high tension between the people making these frequently awkward transitions. That's when it becomes a soap opera.

THE BOARD OF DIRECTORS

Before describing some of the classic soap opera plots that emerge from start-ups, I need to describe another important player in the drama—the board of directors.

The role of the board in public companies has rightfully gotten a lot of scrutiny in the past few years. However, because the boards of start-up companies are not bound by the Sarbanes-Oxley Act and are less likely to have high-priced lawyers and accountants breathing down their necks, they operate quite differently from the large company boards we hear so much about in the news.

The start-up board has both formal and informal duties.[13] Clearly, the primary mission of the board is to increase the value of the equity on behalf of shareholders. In effect, they are agents of the shareholders. In this capacity, they are bound by two important factors: the duty of care (be informed, diligent, and prudent) and the duty of loyalty (serve the interests of the company and its shareholders). The board of directors does not run the company. The CEO runs the company. The best entrepreneurs recognize the important and valuable role that the board can play and provide them with the transparency they need to do their job effectively.

In their capacity as agents for the shareholders, the board of directors has the power to hire and fire the CEO and approve major transactions that materially affect the value of the company's equity, such as selling the company, buying another company, or agreeing to a new round of financing. This role has other important areas of oversight, including serving on the audit committee, which liaises with the company's auditors to confirm the integrity of the financial records and books, or compensation committee, which sets the compensation of the CEO and other senior executives. Through the protective provisions of the term sheet (as described in Chapter 4) the board may have other powers, such as approving major capital expenditures and leases, the issuance of stock option grants, and other major strategic decisions. In short, the board is an important set of advisers to the entrepreneurs, but also a body

---

13. An excellent but not well-known book on this topic is Paul Brountas's *Boardroom Excellence*. Now retired, Paul was a prominent veteran venture capital lawyer in Boston and was secretary of the board at Open Market, where we had the opportunity to work together.

that has an important responsibility to look out for the company and its shareholders, even at the expense of the CEO.

It sounds simple, but it's not. In practice, different shareholders can have different interests, creating competing forces on the board that can cause tension. For one thing, the board members who were selected by the entrepreneur usually have loyalty to him. Even the VC board members are often chosen by the entrepreneur and feel, to a degree, obliged to be supportive of him. That's all well and good when the entrepreneur's interests are perfectly aligned with the shareholder's interests, but sometimes they are not. As Union Square's Fred Wilson put it, "On the one hand, the entrepreneur is a significant shareholder of the company, so your job is to consider what's best for the entrepreneur. But sometimes what's best for the entrepreneur is to move them aside—ideally, in as collaborative a way as possible." The key word is "ideally."

A second tension point is that the board members who are VC investors have a duty of loyalty to the company they funded and a fiduciary duty to that company's shareholders, but they also have a fiduciary duty to their own investors. While sitting on the board of directors, the VC is always weighing how to make their investors the most money possible—that's his job. That may mean trying to invest more VC capital by buying additional equity at a lower price than the price at which the company is willing to sell (see Chapter 4 and the outside-in, inside-out dance). Or it may mean deciding to stop funding the company, thereby driving it out of business. Is that a violation of their duty of loyalty? In truth, it's just a natural tension that exists when you have a board director who has competing fiduciary duties.

And here's where the issue of trust matters so much in the boardroom. The entrepreneurs and the VCs have to trust each other to be open about their motivations. In the case of the entrepreneur, they may be trying to protect their position of power at the expense of shareholder value. In the case of the VCs, they may be trying to achieve gains on behalf of their limited partners at the expense of the other company shareholders. If entrepreneurs and VCs suspect that the hidden motivations of the other are dominating their behavior and their decision making, they will lose trust in their advice and counsel. That's when the soap opera stories begin.

THREE ARCHETYPE DIRECTORS

Board members, like the cast members of a soap opera, tend toward dramatic archetypes. In the case of board members, however, I liken them not to television protagonists like Gregory House from *House* or Jack Bauer from *24*, but to the judges on *American Idol*, a show I thought I would never watch. Only after tuning in for several seasons, and enduring heavy lobbying from my wife, did I become a devotee of the show. What brought me around were not so much the contestants as the judges. I found that I enjoyed listening to Randy, Paula, and Simon (the original judges for many years) as much as I did to the contestants. Maybe more.

One evening as my wife and I watched the show, I began to picture the contestants as entrepreneurs and each of the judges as one of three VC archetypes.

VC Archetype 1: The Domain Expert. Randy Jackson has

worked in the music industry for decades as a performer, producer, and executive with Columbia and MCA. The guy is an expert. His knowledge is palpable when he speaks, and he seems to be very well connected. He displays empathy with the contestants and often gives constructive feedback that is relevant, if a bit limited in scope. Typically, he doesn't focus on the overall strategy, but rather picks out one or two small items to comment on that spring from his great expertise.

Similarly, many entrepreneurs seek out particular VCs to sit on their boards who are deep domain experts and can provide them with expertise relevant to their particular business. Over time, many entrepreneurs find that the domain expert will repeat the same comments over and over and that their solutions are formulaic—"Here's how it's usually done in the industry"—rather than tailored to the specific issues of the company. At the extreme, the deep knowledge of the domain expert can make it more difficult for the entrepreneur to see the big picture of the value creation process.

VC Archetype 2: The Cheerleader. No matter how badly the contestant sings, Paula Abdul, the compassionate judge, always found a way to give them some kind of encouragement. Paula has been down the hard road of making a life as a pop singer and dancer, so she has real empathy for the folks who risk it all and expose themselves to possible ridicule on the show.

Certain VCs display a similar persona in the boardroom. Missed the quarter? Lost a key recruit? "You're doing great," says the cheerleader VC. "Attaboy! Attagirl! Just keep at it. This is hard stuff. We love ya!"

When I was an entrepreneur, I remember one of my board members used to call me or email me with a "Nice job!"

message at the end of every board meeting. At first, I relished it. After ten board meetings and ten "Nice job" emails, I realized I was the recipient of the auto-encouragement message. Cheerleaders can quickly lose credibility and effectiveness.

VC Archetype 3: The Truth Teller. The thing that you love and hate about Simon Cowell is that he tells it like it is. Brutally. Clearly. And he's almost always right.

In the boardroom, the Cowell-like truth-telling VC can give feedback that is tough and hard to hear. "Your sales presentation stunk. You obviously have no idea how to articulate your value proposition." But when you get that rare bit of positive feedback from the truth teller, it's far more meaningful than a hundred happy notes from the cheerleader. "Last quarter was awful, but this quarter you got your act together and executed flawlessly. Well done." You have learned that the truth teller doesn't sugarcoat, so comments like that are precious.

Although the Domain Expert may provide value in assisting with certain valuable introductions and the Cheerleader makes you feel good by telling you what you want to hear, most experienced entrepreneurs will tell you to choose the Truth Teller every time. They develop thick enough skin to value the insight of the Truth Teller and know that they can be trusted to give good, tough advice for even the most complex problems. Board members that hold you accountable force you to elevate your game in ways that would resonate with a good high school basketball coach.

Basketball Hall of Famer and former U.S. Senator Bill Bradley taught me this lesson when he served on our board at Upromise. When we met Bill through one of our investors, we had, fortunately, moved out of my partner's house and were in proper, professional office space. Shortly after his slim loss to Al Gore in the 2000 Democratic presidential primaries, Bill was looking to get involved in a few business ventures. We seemed like a great fit for his interests—education, taxes, the Internet, and entrepreneurship—what could be better?

Having him join our board was a huge honor and thrill for us. Negotiating the details of his compensation package, which fell on my shoulders, was a huge stress for me. How do you say "no" to a few extra tenths of a percentage point of equity to a guy who came within shouting distance of the presidency? But I managed to work out a fair deal, and he was very gracious and wonderful to have on the board.

For his first few board meetings, Bill listened patiently to me as I reported on the ups and downs of our negotiations with the large consumer companies with which we were trying to partner. But finally in one board meeting, Bill had decided he had heard enough.

"Jeff," he interrupted me in his commanding, senatorial voice, "you and Michael have been talking about closing these deals for a few months now. All I want to know is this: With which companies will you have signed contracts by the next board meeting?"

I gulped, feeling the heat of a Senate oversight committee. "Well, I think we'll get Citibank, AT&T . . ."

"Wait a minute," he interrupted me, pulling out his fancy pen and writing on his pad, "Citibank, AT&T. Okay, who else?" he pushed. I gave him a few other names in our pipeline. I don't think I spent a moment over the next thirty days without wondering how the heck I was going to close those contracts we had promised Bill Bradley. Fortunately, we closed them all and launched the service successfully a few months later. One of the partners at Kleiner Perkins remarked to me a few months later, "I've never seen a team so precisely execute on its business development plans so fast." That's probably because the rest of his portfolio didn't have a six-foot, six-inch Bill Bradley breathing down their necks. That's the power of having a Truth Teller on your board.

THREE CLASSIC PLOTS

Of course, I'm being a little facetious with the TV analogy, but not completely. In fact, it's quite useful to think of the start-up as a drama, and the members of the team as characters, so you can quickly recognize important turning points in the plot and, maybe, do something to avert an unhappy ending.

And so, if you'll forgive the TV theme, let me outline the three classic story lines that I've seen played out again and again in start-ups.

Classic Plot 1: Fall from Grace. At the beginning of this show, the CEO—usually the founding entrepreneur—is seen by one and all as the hero of the company, the visionary leader who holds the future in his hands. The VC firm is delighted to be in business with this innovator and crows to its peers, limited partners, and anyone else who will listen to how brilliant the entrepreneur is and how big an impact the company will make.

Then, little by little, things go wrong. The CEO fails to make good on a promise to the board. He misses numbers, reports unforeseen product delays, and has a hard time recruiting top talent. He makes claims that later turn out to be untrue. Makes a weird strategic move. Goes over budget. Provides unpleasant surprises at board meetings or in Friday afternoon emails (why do CEOs always send bad news on Friday afternoon?). Bit by bit, the board members lose trust and confidence in the CEO. They start to wonder if all the information he provides is accurate. They question him more closely and interrogate members of the executive team to gain additional insight. Ultimately, they attempt to put tighter controls on the CEO, spend time in meetings discussing the company's strategy without him, and, suddenly, it feels like the board is trying to manage the company.

At the same time, the CEO feels increasingly under fire. He can't understand why the board, which had told him what a brilliant visionary he was during the honeymoon period, is constantly on his case. The CEO feels they simply don't understand the difficult industry context and factors that are out of his hands. He begins to suspect that some of the board members have a hidden agenda. They want to rein him in, cut him out, or push him in a direction he doesn't want to go. In a panic, he follows a familiar pattern of a CEO in trouble: First, he fires his vice president of sales. ("The guy just can't make the numbers.") Then he fires his vice president of engineering. ("She just couldn't ship the software on time.") Meanwhile, trust erodes on both sides and things begin to fall apart. The CEO and the board stop communicating. The organization becomes dysfunctional. Finally, the CEO is fired, a permanent replacement can't be found quickly or easily, and the company has to be sold prematurely without realizing its full potential.

Unfortunately, I have lived through that drama quite a few

times. The drama is accentuated when the investors themselves have different levels of confidence in the management team. In one of my companies, the largest investor lost faith in the management team and wanted to sell the company. We and the management team wanted to continue to build the business and so undertook a ten-month effort to convince the largest investor to allow us to recapitalize the company and buy them out. The pain and distraction caused the company to miss its numbers for the year and impaired its potential for long-term success. In retrospect, it would have been better if the entrepreneur had never picked that VC as a co-investor or, alternatively, worked harder to ensure alignment of strategy and leadership.

Classic Plot 2: High Noon Shoot-out. In this case, part of the original VC deal is that the company will be run by a professional CEO, approved by the board, and the founder will stay on as a key member of the management team. The founder agrees to this deal in order to secure funding, but never fully buys into the notion that he will need to "let go." From the day the CEO first arrives at the company, it is obvious the two will never get along. The founder questions the CEO's every decision. The CEO wants to change all of the founder's original processes and blames the company's poor performance on the founder's original decisions. The two can't agree on strategy, organization structure, client management, or whom to hire and fire. The founder thinks the CEO is out to wreck the company and will ruin the culture and "soul" he created. The CEO thinks the company can never grow with the founder on the scene looking over his shoulder, looking backward rather than forward.

The board members realize they have to do something, but they're not sure what. Should they fire the CEO? But then how could they ever hire a new CEO when the story of the founder's undermining behavior gets out? Force out the founder? But the founder is the one with the original vision and strategy in which they invested, and often holds critical technical knowledge while the product is still in a very early stage of development. Should they bring in another executive from the outside to mediate—perhaps a part-time chairman? Take a more active role in the day-to-day management themselves? At last, they decide to seek counsel from other members of the management team. At a secret meeting, they call in three of the most senior executives, one by one, and ask for their opinions about what to do. One argues for the CEO. One defends the founder. The third thinks that both should be fired and she should take over.

After much agonizing, the board finally decides that the founder has to go and gives the CEO full authority over the company. Six months later, the CEO abruptly quits. Why? He had lost faith in the board and the mutual trust that existed has eroded. If they agonized so long in their decision to back him this time, what will happen when the next major conflict arises?

I lived through a version of this case, too. Believe me, it was no fun. Worst of all, the drama distracted the senior executive team because they felt compelled to watch the palace intrigue rather than execute the business plan.

Classic Plot 3: VC Mutiny. In this scenario, one or two of the venture capitalists that sit on the board become irritated when the company consistently fails to achieve its performance goals. After being disappointed three quarters in a row, they announce they're going to abandon their investment and leave the board. This forces the other VCs to scramble to find new investors for future rounds of financing in place of the mutineers. The management team has a mild freak-out.

Then, just before the mutinous VCs walk out the door, business picks up. The company exceeds its growth and profit targets for the quarter. The mutineers change their minds. Not only do they stay in, they become much more active and vocal in decision making than they ever had been before. This confuses and disturbs the management team still further. They become resentful and think the board, and this particular VC firm, are unstable and mercurial. Two key executives decide the company is doomed because the board and its relationship with management are tremendously dysfunctional. Those executives leave after getting recruited away to more promising start-ups. Without them, business drops off again. The vocal VCs give up, resurrect their mutiny, write off their investment, and move on to other, more promising start-ups.

You can imagine how distracting these dramas can be in a small, young company. Overcoming technical hurdles, competition, and market uncertainties at start-ups is hard enough. If you have self-inflicted wounds similar to any of these three dramatic plotlines, you are doomed.

AVERTING A FALL FROM GRACE

The best way to avoid such soap operas is for the entrepreneur to be candid and honest with the VCs. The VCs, in turn, must earn the entrepreneur's trust in order for everyone to benefit from this open dialogue.

Dave Balter, founder and CEO of BzzAgent, is as open and transparent an entrepreneur as you will find. When I first met Dave, he was in his early thirties, a visionary guy who had decided that marketing was fundamentally broken. He imagined a new approach that would harness and measure the power of word of mouth. He founded his company, BzzAgent, to deliver on this vision and was able to build it successfully without any institutional capital or help for a number of years.

Dave spent months developing the idea, a word-of-mouth marketing company that would harness the power of conversations among "real" people to launch and promote products and services. He scraped together some money from angel investors—friends and family—and founded BzzAgent in 2002. For three years, with no VC capital, he grew the business from two people to about twenty-five and from nothing to $5 million in annual revenue.

Then, in 2005, Dave hit a wall that is familiar to many start-up founders. He didn't really know how to manage the growth of his company. He saw many possible strategic directions forward but wasn't sure which one to take. He decided he needed help. "For me, the decision to look for capital came down to two things," he said. "One: timing. The business was at the right stage. And, two, I really had no experience. I'd never run a real business. The downside was I would get forced into a quarterly board structure. The upside was that I would learn what CEOs really have to do, how a board thinks about a company, about managing the P&L [profit and loss], and seeing where the challenges really lay. It would be my MBA."

So he raised institutional money to enable his company to grow and selected two VCs to work with (we're one of them) and has partnered with them to build the company into a leader in word-of-mouth marketing. By seeking help and surrounding himself with an experienced board, investors, and management team, Dave has figured out how to grow and build the business in ways that would have been impossible had he relied only on his own ideas and those of his original management team.

At that point, the plot could have twisted into the "CEO falls from grace" scenario, but it didn't. "It was definitely a transition period for me," Dave said. "Post-financing. New executive team. I didn't know what I was supposed to do. For four months, honestly, I'd sit at my desk and say, 'Well, I can't call anyone in sales because I'll step on their toes. I am no longer the one to do the operations stuff.' I actually called one of my VC board members and said, 'Dude, help me! What am I supposed to be doing?'"

Dave started to worry that the board would remove him as CEO. "It's easy to get into that mode in which you live your days thinking, 'Something bad is going to happen to the business. The quarter is going to be off. If I don't do this or that thing right, I'll be canned,'" Dave said. "To be able to succeed, you have to get rid of that fear. You have to focus your thoughts on, 'How is this business going to be awesome?'"

Dave gradually learned to open up and ask the directors for help—indeed, getting help is the reason he did the round of financing in the first place—rather than let the fear overcome him. "I knew I just had to learn how to do all these things differently. Fortunately I'm a sponge, so I'd just get the smartest people in the room to tell me how to do something and then I'd go do it. And so, I was able to let go of thinking that I had to come up with all the answers myself. I realized I don't need to be the smartest guy in the room. I just need to ask, 'Who can solve this? Who can help me do this and show me how?' "

It's pretty obvious when someone is stretching to prove that they're "the smartest guy in the room." VCs and other management team members will conclude that this behavior is an attempt by the entrepreneur to hide their vulnerabilities rather than be open to candid feedback. Establishing the right trusting relationship between the VC and the entrepreneur will avoid many problems down the road.[14]

BEING IN OVER YOUR HEAD

Not all entrepreneurs are as smart as Dave. Many find themselves in the midst of a start-up soap opera and get in way over their heads. I know what that's like. In the early days of my start-up experience at Upromise, I'd sometimes come home at night and tell my wife about the decisions I was wrestling with. I'd shake my head and tell her that I really had no idea what I should be doing. Despite all my experience and education, I felt completely out of my league. What was I doing negotiating a compensation package with Senator Bill Bradley? How could I possibly be sitting in a meeting with Citigroup's then-chairman and former Treasury Secretary Bob Rubin and be

---

14. A great book on this topic is Stephen Covey's *The Speed of Trust*, in which Covey describes why behaviors like "Talk Straight" and "Create Transparency" are core elements in helping to establish trust.

presenting what we do and why it was important for them to become our partner?

I was not alone. Many entrepreneurs sit at their desk or lie awake in bed at night wondering what they're supposed to do and never quite figure it out. But there are many things the entrepreneur can do to take on his new role faster, more successfully, and with less head shaking. Learning to survive and thrive when you're in way over your head is one of the most thrilling parts of the entrepreneurial journey. Here are a few tips I recommend to those who find themselves in this common situation.

Be Honest with Yourself: Following the 80/20 Rule

It's almost impossible for an entrepreneur *not* to get in over his head, especially in the early stages of building a company. The key is to know when you're in over your head in a healthy and challenging way and when you're in so far you're in danger of getting overwhelmed. One entrepreneur suggests applying the 80/20 rule. You're in good shape if you feel in command of the business about 80 percent of the time and sitting in your office wondering what to do only about 20 percent of the time. It's the 20 percent stretch that makes the work fun and challenging. But if you're in the reverse situation, scratching your head 80 percent of the time and in command only 20 percent? Not good.

When you realize you're on the wrong side of the 80/20 rule, don't hide it. Admit it. Talk openly about it with your board and management team. Serial entrepreneur Tim Bucher, formerly vice president of engineering at Apple and co-founder of

WebTV and Zing Systems, explained it to me, "Look, I'm just a simple farm boy. [Tim grew up on a farm in northern California before earning his engineering degree at UC Davis.] I have to work hard to sound intelligent. But I'd look forward to board meetings. I needed the help and wanted the advice."

But it's not always easy to know how deeply over your head you are. You're in a new situation, doing things you've never done before, and sometimes you hardly recognize yourself at all. That's why I often encourage my portfolio CEOs to retain an executive coach. The coach should be an outsider, not a board member, and somebody who can act as the CEO's confidential sounding board and also a sounding board for the directors, if that becomes necessary. I also recommend CEOs insist that their board complete an annual, written performance review and solicit input for it from all board members and management team members. This process forces the CEO to be self-aware and the board to be open about any concerns they might have.

Get Help

Another important piece of advice to entrepreneurs running companies is to seek the advice of the wise men and women around you to learn how to step up and grow into the situation in which you find yourself. Don't close yourself off to outside advice for fear of appearing weak. Instead, embrace smart, diverse opinions to help shape your own.

Dave Balter, for example, relied heavily on the advice of Shikhar Ghosh, an experienced entrepreneur and one of his angel investors (and chairman and founder of Open Market), especially during the process of choosing a VC firm. "The smartest thing I did was get Shikhar to help," Dave said. "He knew the players, knew where they play and where they don't play, and could teach me what to do. And, frankly, when I look back, I was kind of a puppet in that process. I played my role, which was to be the overworked entrepreneur, too busy to really care about the financing. My attitude was, 'I love all you guys, let's do whatever you want!' Shikhar played the straight man, saying, 'This is how we're going to do the deal and this is how it's going to work.'"

Many entrepreneurs are terrible at asking for help and just as bad at accepting it, even if they do seek it. After all, they have become entrepreneurs because they enjoy being their own boss and are passionate and often stubborn about following their vision. It's hard for them to admit they need help and that, sometimes, they need a life preserver to pull them out of whatever situation they're in.

The advice the entrepreneur may get—from his advisers or his board—is that it's time to hire a chief operating officer to work with him, or hire a CEO and move into the chairman's role, or to make some other move that involves ceding some amount of control to other people.

Christoph Westphal had a great perspective on this when we talked about his management challenges at Sirtris. "At the end of the day, and this is a mistake all of us make as founders or entrepreneurs, it's not our company, even if we are the founders. It's not the venture capitalists' company. It's not the management's company. It's a company that we want to be successful no matter what. For example, I want to always find someone who is better than me to replace me in whatever I'm doing. So I've just hired a COO who's better than me at running Sirtris."

Reid Hoffman at LinkedIn had a similar experience. Although he served as the founding CEO during the early years, Reid helped recruit a CEO to run the day-to-day operations as the company scaled in size. With a new CEO in place, Reid is able to focus on strategy and vision and let someone else focus on building the machine. Surrounding yourself with the right help is a critical skill for entrepreneurs who want to scale their businesses beyond their own personal abilities and efforts.

Manage the Board Before It Manages You

Gail Goodman, CEO of Constant Contact, has a lot of experience managing a board of directors.

"The single most important thing to do with a board is to keep them really up to date on the business," Gail said. "The good *and* the bad. Constantly focusing them on the next very small milestones and the very simple metrics that will demonstrate success at each one of them. In our business, it was how many trials are we generating? What is our trial-to-pay conversion rate? What is our attrition rate? What is our retention rate? We wanted to be unbelievably clear about what was working and what wasn't working, then asking for advice and listening to the good parts."

And that brings up a downside of asking for help. A good board—filled with domain experts, truth tellers, and cheerleaders—will give you far more advice, some of it conflicting, than you need or can ever use. "That's a little bit of a secret with boards," Gail told me. "They will run you ragged with ideas. They'll have a million ideas and they'll be all over the place. Sometimes they'll get upset if you don't take them all. The solution to that is board alignment and a high frequency of communication. So, when we were doing board meetings every six weeks, I was talking to each director between the board meetings. They always knew exactly what was going on, what was working, what wasn't working, which ideas I was pursuing and which ones I wasn't. I was very honest with them."

"No secrets. No surprises," Dave Balter explained. "I heard that early as a CEO. If something new is going to come up in a board meeting that's not good, put the calls out early to the directors. 'Here's what's going on, here's why. I want you to think about it. Help me.' So when we get in the board meeting, they don't say, 'What are you talking about?'"

Gail made a point of previewing news with each director right before the board meeting to allow them to have some reflection time before the meeting, and to alert her to any of their initial concerns. "I wanted them to know exactly what they were going to hear in the meeting. By the time we got into the board meeting, everybody was informed and we could really get into the meat of whatever the issue was."

The "no surprises" rule applies to changes in management as well as performance metrics. "The board would lose confidence in some team members at different times," Gail told me. "So I was very clear about saying, 'I see the same weaknesses. But here's what they're doing. And I'll make the decision about this person at the right time.' You can't fool these guys. If you have an executive that has weaknesses and you try to deny it, it erodes the board's confidence, makes them think you don't have good judgment when it comes to people. So you've got to be honest, but you've also got to do what's right for you and the business. I'd say, 'I share your concerns. But, right now, here is the role this person is playing. I need her. You don't want me working on a transition in that role when this more urgent problem needs my attention, do you?'"

This kind of management of the directors is especially important for the first several meetings of the board, because the directors, too, are trying to figure out their roles and how they can be most effective. As Gail said, "Early on, there can be a fair amount of grandstanding. Each director has to prove they have an insight. By preparing right, we got into working the issues much faster. So I would say that you cannot over-invest in board management. In the early days, I estimate I spent fifteen to twenty percent of my time managing my board—seeking their advice, preparing for the meetings, following up on action items. I needed it. Because I was going to need their money."

Each director plays an important role as an individual and, collectively, the board can be very helpful, or very detrimental. The best entrepreneurs give a lot of thought and attention to these roles, knowing how to harness the talent around them to achieve the best results for the company.

THE LONGEST-RUNNING SHOWS ARE ENSEMBLES

The most successful start-ups operate like good ensembles. The attitude is, "We're all in this together. We don't want to upstage each other. We want to make each other look good. We want to put on a really great show."

Fred Wilson of Union Square Ventures has an interesting take on the relationship between the entrepreneur and the venture capitalist. "I think venture capitalists, first and foremost, need to feel like their job is to make entrepreneurs successful. So I think of venture capital as a service business. The entrepreneur is your client. It's a very weird relationship because the entrepreneur is not exactly paying you, even though they really are paying you. But they absolutely can't fire you. In fact, you can fire them. So it's among the weirdest kinds of service relationships that one could come up with."

"Every financing is an argument in which you try to think about the long-term health of the company," Christoph Westphal of Sirtris told me. "There are shared interests among the players. Management, independent board member, angel, and venture folk. A lot of entrepreneurs get it wrong. They think, 'The venture guys are trying to take advantage.' But, no, they have a job to do. They're trying to make money, because they actually need to make money to make this reasonable. Everyone is in the same boat. There are diverse interests. But on a path toward success as a profitable company, ultimately, the people who understand that everyone is in it together are going to be the ones who understand that there is an alignment of incentives."

The importance of the ensemble approach is important for assembling and leading a management team as well as a board. Entrepreneurs who want to succeed must be great at recruiting cast members and directing them in a coordinated, harmonious fashion.

6

JACKPOT: ROUTES TO CASHING OUT

A book about starting new companies wouldn't be complete without a discussion of the ending—the exit or cash-out. For the VC, the exit is a routine part of the job. You invest your limited partners' money and expect to get a good return back for it after a number of years. The profile of an investment in a start-up company is a fairly unique one. Most other investment vehicles are relatively liquid: the investor can sell his stake or shares at almost any time. An investment in a start-up company, however, is very, *very* illiquid. For the VC, investing in these young companies feels a bit like the Eagles song about staying at the Hotel California: "You can check out anytime you like, but you can never leave." At some point, the VC needs to leave.

For the entrepreneur, the exit is an emotional roller coaster. They are selling their baby. They may forever change their lifestyle and succeed in providing for their family's future. Or they may miss out on their small and closing window of opportunity to cash out big. This difference in emotional makeup reminds me of the old joke about how committed the pig and the chicken are to the farmer's breakfast of eggs and bacon. When it comes to selling your business, the VC is like the chicken—interested in the outcome, but not nearly as committed as the entrepreneur, who is like the pig—about to become the bacon.

VCs typically get their investment capital back by selling their shares in one of two ways: by taking the company public in an initial public offering (IPO) or by selling the company to another entity—usually another company, but it could also be another group of investors—for cash or stock.

Despite all the attention that IPOs get in the press (and the investor's imagination), it is by far the less common cashout method for a venture capitalist. Each year, approximately 1,000-1,500 new companies receive VC funding, but only 2-3 percent of them achieve an IPO.[15] The requirements for a company to go public are onerous. It must have predictable revenue (which usually means north of $50 million in annual sales, sometimes as much as $100 million), rising profits, and mature systems and processes that allow it to be in compliance with Sarbanes-Oxley and other relevant legislation, as defined by the SEC.[16] According to the NVCA, venture-backed start-ups that go public typically are ten years old. To reach those financial milestones and achieve that "overnight" success is a rarity

15. NVCA 2009 Yearbook.
16. The Sarbanes-Oxley Act, passed in 2003 in the wake of Enron, WorldCom, Tyco, and other accounting scandals, is the bane of the successful start-up. Designed for the Fortune 500, this onerous regulation has made it very difficult for companies to go public, costing $2 million to $3 million per year in compliance expenses. Congress desperately needs to reform this legislation in order to facilitate the continued growth of the innovation economy. End of rant.

in the world of start-ups. At my former company, Open Market, we were lucky to go public during the market's heyday in 1996. It seemed so easy to me back then. The company was barely two years old and had no systematic business processes, few customers, little revenue, and nascent technology. At our IPO party, one of the wise old hands put his arm around my shoulder and laughed at me. "Jeff," he said, "you have no idea how rare this is and how lucky we are. This sort of thing just doesn't happen." Boy, was he right. Thirteen years later, I still haven't attended another IPO party.

Even when a company does succeed in going public, the IPO usually does not do for the entrepreneur what most of them would like—it does not mean an immediate exit for them or even a monster "liquidity event." The IPO, instead, usually brings new challenges and stresses. Suddenly, the entrepreneur must be accountable to a new cast of characters, in addition to the board of directors. Public company shareholders, in particular, can be even tougher to deal with than the toughest VC. And there are onerous restrictions on selling your shares as a company insider and visible leader.

I remember, for example, when I made a presentation in my role as vice president of marketing at the first event we held for investors just after we took Open Market public. A shareholder got up and asked, "If your company is so great and your prospects so promising, could you explain why your CEO sold ten thousand shares of stock last week?" Ouch. Entrepreneurs are now more aware that once that company goes public, whenever they sell a share in their company, the information is made public and easily available online. In another investor meeting, after delivering my presentation to the larger audience,

I retired to a smaller, "private" group for Q&A. That evening I flew home and found a transcript of my Q&A session posted publicly on the Yahoo! message board. After those two experiences, I made a note to myself: Don't ever become a public company CEO. It's not as glamorous as it seems.

EXIT CONSIDERATIONS: WHO, WHAT, WHEN, AND HOW

So let's put the IPO scenario aside for now (I'll return to it later in the chapter and share the case studies of Gail Goodman at Constant Contact and Christoph Westphal at Sirtris and their IPO successes). Instead, let's focus on the main mechanism for hitting the jackpot: selling your company to another company.

How to sell your company is a tricky mix of considerations. Many serial entrepreneurs will tell you that they think about the exit the moment they enter. In fact, the "exit strategy" is one of the main considerations VCs analyze before they make an investment in a start-up. The entrepreneur and VC should think about and talk about the various appropriate exit candidates very early on in the process: "If we build this, who would want to buy it?" With these buyers in mind, the entrepreneur should then endeavor to get on the radar screen of the relevant executives of the potential acquirers as early as possible. Either through business development partnerships, joint customer work, competitive wins, or simply mingling at industry conferences, getting to know the people who might someday buy your company and letting them get to know you is a critical ingredient for navigating to a successful exit.

The other important conversation to have with your VC partners very early on is what their expectations are for the exit. Ideally, this is a conversation you have with them before they even invest. Are they looking for a five-times return or a ten-times return? Would they sell out at $100 million? One billion? Or in the case of Jack Dorsey's Twitter and Reid Hoffman's LinkedIn, would they wait until something closer to $10 billion? This dialogue about numbers and expectations needs to continue throughout the life of the company. After almost every board meeting, many VCs walk out with a notion of the number rattling around in their heads for how much they would sell this company today and the number at which they hope to sell the company in a few years. These numbers and the thinking behind them should be openly discussed by all sides at all times.

When to sell can be the hardest question the entrepreneur faces. There is no easy answer as it depends so much on the entrepreneur's personal interests and the state of the business. Here are five considerations that help frame the decision:

1. Do you still love running the business? Does it feel like you can't imagine doing anything else with your life? Do you still feel like you have something to prove or do you feel tired and worn out?

2. Do you still believe passionately in the business's potential? Does it appear that the major proof points are still ahead of the company?

3. How much is the offer as compared to what it might be a year or two from now if the company were to successfully execute on its plan and hit its numbers? What might the

company's value be in a year or two if it falls short of its plan by 30 percent? How would you assess the probability of either path and then calculate the expected value of holding on for a few more years as compared to taking the money off the table by selling now?

4. Does the business require more capital and, if so, can that additional capital be raised easily at a reasonable (and therefore not too dilutive) price?

5. Do the people around you (i.e., your management team, your VCs, your family) want you to sell out or are they encouraging you to keep going?

Fred Wilson of Union Square Ventures captured this tension well when we talked about a start-up he backed where the older, wiser, more seasoned entrepreneurs took the money. "The founders got a hundred-million-dollar offer, which would mean tens of millions for them personally. I could see it in their eyes. Their wives were saying, 'Take the money.' And I totally respected it. They have kids, they have wives, mortgages, lives. And it was enough money that all of those guys were never going to have to have a day job that they didn't want to have ever again. That's what happens, I think, when you get into your thirties and even in your forties. I think that sometimes it's harder to throw caution to the wind and go for it, just outright go for it."

This tension between selling early and "going for it" is a fundamental one that all successful entrepreneurs face. On the one hand, I personally love working with entrepreneurs who have already made some money (the sweet spot seems to be $2-5 million), where they have enough tucked away to feel safe taking bigger risks but not so much that they've lost their hunger and drive. On the other hand, there are numerous stories of entrepreneurs who didn't sell at the right time and ended up with a fraction of what they could have had. Finding the right time to sell is a delicate process with multiple emotional and rational factors at play, as the next case study demonstrates.

A CASE STUDY IN FINDING THE RIGHT MOMENT TO SELL

I told the early part of the Brontes story in Chapter 3—about how Eric Paley and Micah Rosenbloom teamed up with MIT researchers to commercialize an imaging system for dentistry applications, particularly for replacing the messy impressions that have been required for making crowns.

Eric's exit was also full of strategic shifts and reversals of fortune. This story is complicated a bit (or enriched, depending on how you look at it) by the fact that I was on the Brontes board at the time and so I'm going to tell the story from both perspectives: mine and Eric's.

By mid-2006, the company was ready to move into its next phase. The team had spent two years working on the technology and the application, a process that had been pretty trying for everybody involved. But now, with some of the kinks worked out, it was time to move decisively into the commercialization period, coupled with a sales and marketing effort. Building a manufacturing operation and hiring a sales team would be an expensive endeavor. Eric and Micah calculated that we would need another $15 million to complete the final product and then an additional $20 million to get to cash flow breakeven.

Meanwhile, the company was running out of money, having consumed nearly all of the $10 million of capital it had raised to date. We needed to raise money. Fast.

This prospect, naturally, made us all very uneasy—especially Eric. In our discussions, he learned that I and the other investors were hesitant to continue funding the company alone given the large amount of additional capital required to achieve breakeven. And, even if we did, how would we agree to a price? On the one hand, the technology appeared to work and showed great promise. But on the other hand, the team had consistently missed major development milestones and had a long way to go.

"Yeah, we were supposed to prove that we could actually image something by the end of 2005," Eric said. "We did have a beta device in December. But it didn't work. For a whole week nothing worked, and we were saying, 'Oh my God!' We had spent over a year trying to get to this point, and we started to feel we were never going to get there. But at last we got the beta working and showed it to the board. They were satisfied to see something, but they were terribly concerned about how far it was from a product we could take into a clinic."

With some of the major technical hurdles behind it, the company felt like it was on a roll. Eric believed that the company's value had greatly increased since the initial round of funding, largely because of the positive feedback the Brontes technology had garnered at the Chicago Mid-Winter Dental Meeting in February 2006, one of the biggest dental conventions in the United States. "They said it couldn't be done and tonight we saw it," declared the president of a large dental lab who had been shown the product. Eric came back from

Chicago on a high and told us that the value of the business had skyrocketed. Although we agreed, we were unsure whether it would be enough to get someone from the outside to invest in the company given how much longer we had to go.

Not long after the Chicago show, Eric and I got together for dinner in Harvard Square, in Cambridge, to talk about where we were. "It was a terribly uncomfortable dinner," Eric remembered with a wince. Here I was telling him that the investors were nervous that we didn't have enough capital around the table to take the company the whole way. That said, we would invest some more money in the company, but Eric didn't like the price that we felt was a fair one. You can imagine the tension: Eric was a sitting CEO, running out of cash, coming to the board—that sets his compensation and has the power to fire him—and he was being prickly in negotiating the price and terms for the new money.

After that dinner we had together, Eric kept thinking about how to demonstrate the value of the company to us and prospective outside investors. "I knew all the key potential acquirers in the industry. If one of them was to offer thirty million dollars for our business, that would go a long way in demonstrating that the company's value had appreciated. I thought we had a real chance of getting an offer. I told you, perhaps stretching, that I thought we could get as much as sixty million within the next year. And you were sort of shocked that I said that."

Compounding Eric's need to prove the value of the company were his concerns about proving he could handle the job. From before we had invested in Brontes, Eric and I discussed the likelihood that at some point we would bring in a CEO with sales and marketing experience. This prospect, naturally, made Eric very uneasy. Eric admitted, "I had the insecurity and ego of a first-time CEO, feeling the whole time like I'm going to get fired after every board meeting. And thinking, 'When are they going to put in some guy I hate to run the company?'"

For Eric, it seemed to be a do-or-die moment. He had to embark on the inside-out, outside-in dance while trying to keep the company moving forward. And all with the specter of running out of cash and perhaps being replaced down the road hanging over him. "I figured if a new CEO was going to come in, no matter what, he would get huge equity," Eric said. "I had all these fears about how badly I was going to be diluted, and how the new CEO wouldn't really care that much about the previous shareholders. If I was really going to be replaced, I had very little protection. So I wanted to get the best valuation and terms I could for myself and the common shareholders."

Fortunately, we had established a very open relationship and the entrepreneurs and the board trusted each other. Even though the issues confronting us were difficult ones, we were direct in how we communicated them. "I knew that I had the kind of board members who would not screw me or the company," Eric said. "They weren't necessarily going to do everything they could to maximize my personal equity interest in the company, but they certainly would never sabotage the business. We were able to get to an agreement where they put me in a strong position to raise money. I could go out and say, 'The insider investors want this round, but there's a price. If you exceed that price, they'll let an outsider lead it. If not, the inside investors will simply continue forward.'"

To get the highest valuation possible, Eric thought it made sense to talk not only with outside VCs but also with potential strategic partners—that is, large companies that operated in the dental industry. "I had this idea that a strategic partner might pay the highest price," Eric said. "It would give us some insight into whether there was really an acquirer out there at this stage. How interested are these parties? Where are they really? So we went out to three companies we knew in the industry. All of them were interested."

So Eric approached a number of VC institutions as well as the three industry players, including the ultimate buyer, 3M. "When the outside VC term sheets came in they were really disappointing," Eric bemoaned. "People spent tons of time on due diligence and then came in with what I felt were really weak offers. They offered terms that our insiders would have matched or beaten."

I had mixed feelings when I saw these offers from the other potential VC investors. On the one hand, they validated our excitement for the company as well as our views on the appropriate pricing for the next round of financing. On the other hand, the low offers meant we were stuck with continuing to finance the business without additional help for the next few years.

The strategic offers from the industry players, though, were really good. Even better than we had hoped. Ultimately, we got a good valuation for the financing from a strong industry player. We went back to the other strategic partners and said, "We're done."

But they weren't done. "One of the other players said, 'No, no. We're coming up to see you,'" Eric recounted. "We had dinner and they said, 'What can we do to convince you? We'll beat the other guy's price.' I said, 'Look, let's be blunt. Because of who you are, taking an investment from you will compromise our long-term business. With the other player we're selecting, it's not an issue. So, there's just no price at which we're going to take investment dollars from you. The only way you get into this business is if you want to buy it. And we don't see that happening because it would be an absurd amount of money relative to the fact that we have no revenue. So, we really don't think that's practical."

Eric was skillfully playing a negotiating game, and fortunately for him and us, the game still wasn't over. Nothing spurs a prospective acquirer like walking away, especially when you are walking away because of a competitive alternative. Creating scarcity is one of the most powerful tools in an exit negotiation.

So, the second player went to its board and called Eric the following week. They told Eric, "We want to put an offer down to buy the company, but we don't know how much yet. We're trying to figure it out. How much are you guys thinking about?"

A classic move. The potential acquirer doesn't want to name a number because if it's higher than what the seller is looking for, there's no way to go lower. If they start low, however, they can always increase the offer. But the seller doesn't want to name a number either. "You don't want to put a low price because you might undersell yourself," Eric said. "But you don't want to make it so high that they say, 'Oh my God, that's so insane. There's no way.'"

With a committed Series B financing, Eric had a credible

alternative to selling the company. He was able to say to the bidder, "We're going to tell you the numbers from our planned financing. We're not going to sell for less than where our current investors value the business, which is $75 million. If you want to talk about a premium to that, let's talk. If you don't, let's not."

The first offer came in at $55 million—hardly the premium to the valuation that Eric was looking for. But Eric and Micah then shopped the offer to every company that they had shown the "movie" of Brontes 3D to over the past two years. These companies had become educated enough that they were uncomfortable with the idea that a competitor might end up owning the company. When four additional industry players came in, it became an auction, and the deal finally closed at $95 million. "It was neat because the board allowed management to choose the acquirer," Eric said. "And the sale was not just based on the price. We chose the right acquirer for us and we were able to push them to the right price. Was there money left on the table? We'll never know. Probably money is always left on the table. But you're dealing with risk against return. If we had gone higher, the other players might have left the table. And then you start losing leverage in negotiating. It can unwind as quickly as it winds."

The story's ending was a happy one for everyone. Even though Brontes had still not finished the product or taken in a penny of revenue, 3M was happy as the winning bidder because the acquisition allowed it to exclusively own an incredibly innovative product that had the potential to transform the industry. We, the investors, were happy to realize a significant return on our investment in a relatively short period of time.

Eric and his partner, Micah Rosenbloom, were happy to both cash out and stay on as the leaders of the business unit, thus escaping their fear of being replaced and not seeing the venture through to the end. And all of us, you included, will soon have a much more pleasant experience when your dentist needs to take an image of your teeth.

The two lessons for me that jump out of the Brontes case study are (1) the importance of transparency and trust between the VC and the entrepreneur, particularly during a process as sensitive as the exit; and (2) having a solid funding alternative, which is a huge advantage when talking to potential acquirers. The open, trusting relationship Eric had with me and the other board members allowed us to navigate through tricky issues and smoothly resolve the complex decision of when and how to sell. And the fact that there was another, viable financing path for the company to pursue in the event that the sale price was not good enough allowed Eric to fulfill the old adage, "companies are bought, not sold."

A BUMPY ROAD TO AN IPO

Although the IPO is a rarity, it is worth describing in some detail as it is so special an opportunity for an entrepreneur to realize her dreams. In Chapter 3, I introduced Gail Goodman, CEO of Constant Contact, and her considerable management and entrepreneurial skills. She and her company traveled a pretty bumpy road from her arrival as CEO in 1999 to IPO in 2007. Gail led her management team through three rounds of financing. The first two involved pitching to over a hundred

VC firms, and they suffered some pretty rough treatment at the hands of both VCs and banks. But the story has a happy ending. Constant Contact raised $107 million in its October 2007 IPO, with the stock price rising as high as $28.01 on its debut day, well above its forecast range of $12–14. Today, the company is the leader in its market space and has a market capitalization of over $500 million.

When Gail joined the nascent company—then called Roving Software—that serial entrepreneur Randy Parker had founded, she was focused on taking on a new challenge and having a shot at being in the corner office. She had spent most of her career in high-technology management in more established companies. After earning her MBA from the Amos Tuck School at Dartmouth, she joined consulting firm Bain & Company and then worked at four midsized, high-growth software companies, most recently serving as a vice president at Open Market. She then began to feel the entrepreneurial itch.

Meanwhile, Randy had been trying to raise money for Roving Software, with little luck, for about a year before Gail arrived on the scene. The VCs liked the idea, but wanted to see him paired up with an experienced business executive. Then Randy met a group of angel investors who agreed to put in $400,000—and also found him a CEO, Gail Goodman.

When Gail came on board, the company had seven employees. "The company had no product, no revenue," she remembers. "It had something it was calling a beta that was more of an alpha. But I had a lot of confidence in the basic idea that Randy had—email marketing for small business."

Like many entrepreneurs who get hired to run an existing, young business, the reality of the situation was less rosy than the investor's recruiting pitch. Gail quickly discovered that the company had consumed most of the seed funding Randy had cobbled together. "I thought there was way more of a cash runway than there actually was. The first week I got there, I was like, 'We have how many weeks of cash left?' "

So Gail started fund-raising immediately. "We had a lot of things going against us. We didn't have a sweet spot in the market. It was still the world of enterprise software with million-dollar deals the norm. We were saying, 'We're going to sell our product for thirty dollars a month.' Plus, the idea of 'software as a service' didn't really exist yet."

Gail pitched forty firms looking for a first round of VC investment. "I was a first-time CEO. It was my first time raising money. First-time everything. What befuddled me was that I was pitching a very practical and reasonable growth trajectory, but everybody kept telling me, 'Oh no, that's not aggressive enough. It's got to be $100 million in three years or we're not interested.' I had passion for the business and great credibility. But the truth was that we had no idea how quickly the business was going to ramp up. So, if the VCs wanted me to be more aggressive about near-term trajectory in order for them to be interested, so be it. But it was not comfortable for me."

Eventually, Gail convinced two VCs to believe enough in her and the business vision to raise $10 million.

Over the next three years, Constant Contact completed its product, won customers, and began to make money. But as they ramped up quickly, they burned through the $10 million faster than they had intended. Meanwhile, the macroeconomic environment was deteriorating. The Internet bubble had burst and VCs got very skittish about investing in online businesses.

During that time, Constant Contact had all the classic start-up company issues. One of Gail's VCs, who had a lot of experience with early-stage companies, reacted very differently from the other, who was much more used to helping later-stage companies scale up and get ready to go public. "As we hit potholes, the first VC was like, 'Nothing new under the sun!'" Gail said. "While the other was always going, 'The sky is falling! We're doomed!'"

In 2002, Gail set out to raise another $5 million in financing and approached her reluctant VCs for participation. But, shaken by tough market conditions, they had decided to shut down some of their underperforming portfolio companies rather than reinvest. So relations turned tense. "We were working with a junior partner in their East Coast office," Gail said, "but the center of power was on the West Coast. So we were told to come to the New York office and do a video conference presentation to the guys in California. They were the ones who had the power to say thumbs-up or thumbs-down. Well, we get into the room, get linked up on video, and we see that the two key West Coast decision makers aren't even there. As soon as I start presenting, two-thirds of the people in the West Coast office get up and walk out of the room."

Despite this rude behavior, and in large part thanks to Gail's powers of persuasion, both firms continued forward while two new VCs came on board, and Constant Contact snagged another $5 million. Unfortunately, the new money came in the form of a recapitalization round at a much lower price than previous rounds of financing. As often happens during a recapitalization—or "down round"—the founder, Randy Parker, got heavily diluted. "He got squashed," Gail said with a grimace.

"The board didn't re-up him with incremental stock options the way they re-upped the rest of the executives."

Unfortunately for Randy, founders often play a less critical role over time as a company matures. As such, they can be at risk of getting squeezed out if a company gets refinanced at a lower price than the previous round, thereby suffering meaningful dilution. The VCs typically protect the going-forward management team from such dilution, but not the founder unless the founder is still considered essential to the business.

Back to Constant Contact—with four VCs around the table to manage, Gail had the challenge of getting everyone aligned about what to do next. "Everybody was in a different mind-set because of what was going on with their portfolios," Gail said. "Two people wanted to put more money in and step on the gas. Two people were nervous and wanted more proof points. So we had this debate."

The debate continued throughout 2003 and 2004. VCs are very skilled at deferring decisions, sometimes too skilled. When I transitioned from the entrepreneurial side over to the VC side, I quickly learned why. VCs think about time very differently than entrepreneurs. For VCs, time is your friend. The more time you have to make a decision, the more information you get and the better-quality decision you think you can make. For entrepreneurs, time is your enemy. Entrepreneurs have a huge sense of urgency—urgency to get ahead of their competition, urgency to fulfill customer promises, urgency to make payroll as cash runs out. Meanwhile, no matter how bad things get in their portfolio, VCs always return to their cushy offices and collect their management fees the next Monday, even after shutting down a company.

Gail is an entrepreneur who always operates with a sense of huge urgency, and so despite this mismatch with her VCs, she kept her head down and kept executing her plan to build the business. In 2005, Constant Contact began to run on all cylinders. The company doubled its revenue from the previous year to $15 million, and was projecting to double again in 2006. But still no decision from the VCs about additional financing. Gail was getting frustrated.

Around that time, Gail was contacted by Bill Kaiser of Greylock, one of the nearly hundred venture capitalists who had originally turned her down, but had been hearing about the company's momentum. "It was a very funny email. I saved it. He wrote, 'Let me be one of the many Boston VCs who are humbly returning to say, having turned you down, that we were so wrong. Can we have lunch?'" They had lunch and Kaiser offered to put a term sheet together, something Gail could use as a catalyst to get her deadlocked board to finally make a decision.

She made a presentation to her investors explaining her plan to raise additional capital. "I said, 'We're going to raise this capital from Greylock and, after we've raised it, we're going to spend it and that's going to make us unprofitable. But it's about marketing and securing lifetime customer revenue and here's how the math works.'"

Her first presentation was to one of the originally reluctant VCs. "Now it was like a love fest," Gail said. "Because we had reached the stage they really know about. They know how to scale. So now they're saying, 'Oh, you've done a great job with this business, blah-blah-blah. And why are you only raising five million? We've got to capitalize this business the right way.' Finally we're in their sweet spot. It was inspirational."

The exit discussion intensified. One of the investors believed that the company should cash out in 2006. "Their theory was that the right time to sell a company is when it has between twenty-five and forty million in revenue," Gail said. "That's when you're the prettiest. And there's a whole new risk in scaling up to the next level." Such a sale to a larger company would have likely yielded somewhere between $100 million and $150 million in value—a nice return for the investors, but not the bigger payout Gail knew she could achieve if she could keep growing the business. Gail's confidence in her own business model, and the support of enough of her investors around the table, encouraged her to keep going and pursue an IPO "exit" rather than a strategic sale.

But cashing out is never solely an exercise in economics; there is a strong emotional aspect to it. "If we had not been ready to go public, we were going to have to think about selling the company," Gail said. "And that was depressing to all of us. Unlike some companies, there was nobody on our team who said, 'I'm getting tired.' Quite the contrary. We were just getting the resources to do all this cool stuff, getting the channel where we wanted it, achieving scale. We had a vision of everything we wanted to do. Besides, we looked at the set of people who might buy us and we thought, 'They'll break it. There's no way they're going to understand what we've done!' We, however, knew exactly what we wanted to do. We believed we were creating a sustainable, independent brand. Small businesses need a full suite of things to help them manage company relationships. And we thought we were the right guys to do it. So we just had too much passion around what we wanted to do. Nobody was in a hurry to sell."

So late that year, Gail started talking with bankers and, by the early part of 2007, the bankers determined that an IPO could happen that fall. "You need to have certain proven economics," said Gail. "We knew we would do $50 million in 2007. We were going to cross into EBITDA [earnings before interest, taxes, depreciation, and amortization] profitability in the second half of the year. The business felt like it was at the right scale. It was mature enough. We had the executive team. Markets were open, and you never know how long they stay open."

Gail and her team then began preparing for the IPO. After a grueling road show, consisting of over sixty presentations in sixteen nonstop days, the IPO was scheduled to take place on Wednesday, October 3. The price range set by the bankers was $12–14 per share. That morning, Gail and her team gathered in the kitchen of Constant Contact's office. "IPOs don't trade at the opening bell," Gail told me. "There is a separate desk at the stock exchange where they balance the buy and sell orders, which is all done by hand the first day. So we're all in the kitchen back at the office waiting for the first trade. We had a live feed from the trading floor, but we knew we wouldn't hear anything until ten-thirty or so. Finally, my cell phone goes off. 'We can't balance the book,' they tell me. 'It'll be another ten minutes.' Okay, we're all still calm but excited. A second call comes in. 'We still can't balance the book,' I hear. 'It'll be another ten minutes.' I say, 'What's going on?' They say, 'We can't talk now' and hang up. We all wait another forty minutes. We're stuffed in the kitchen. It's getting really hot. None of us know what's going on. I've never done this before. I don't have a clue. And then we get the call. The first trade is at twenty-six dollars—more than twice what we expected. Pandemonium, just pandemonium. Champagne started arriving, flowers started arriving. And we're exhausted, coming off the IPO road show. I was as beat as I've ever been in my life. So I was just sitting in my office like dead meat, watching stuff come in, taking phone calls. Everybody going, 'I never dreamed! I never dreamed!'"

One thing that impressed me most about my meeting with Gail in our interview for this book was that, two years after the IPO, she had not lost one iota of energy and passion for what she was doing. "We have the most fun business in the world," she gushed. "Our customers love us. It's so easy to make them happy. We add so much value to their business. They can't believe how cheap the product is. So the customers are fun and working with the customers is fun. The upside is still ahead of us, and we're having a blast."

Gail has it figured out. The IPO is an important event in the life of a company, but the best entrepreneurs don't really view it as an "exit." It may be an exit for the VCs and other early investors, but the best entrepreneurs view it as nothing more than a financing event (albeit a very public one) and keep pursuing the upside that is still ahead of them.

IPO, THEN SELL

Now that we've covered case studies on the two most typical exits—a strategic sale and an IPO—let's review an unusual case that involved both.

Christoph Westphal (profiled in Chapter 2) pursued a two-step exit path. First, he took his company Sirtris public in 2007. Then he sold the company to GSK for $720 million a year after his IPO. Christoph explained to me that, like Eric Paley, he courted his potential acquirers throughout the company's history—even earlier than some of his board members wanted him to.

"Merck, Pfizer, GSK, they all started calling me, wanting to meet," Christoph explained. "My investors were nervous that I would reveal too much, but my attitude was, 'They're a huge company. It will take them five years to get organized. We are way ahead of them.'" So Christoph took the meetings, briefed them at a high level on the firm's progress, and even published many of their early research findings.

Even while raising increasingly large sums of money from VCs and other private sources, Christoph began to lay the groundwork to take the company public—something he was keen to do rather than sell out too early to the large pharmaceutical companies that were courting him. As an experienced VC, he knew that preparing to take a company public has a long lead time. "Getting the IPO done was a two-year process. I was in New York every month meeting with institutions, telling them our story. When it was time for the road show, I had met with most of them five times. Even though the story was still very early and a bit crazy, they saw our progress and trusted us."

In early 2006, Christoph saw the IPO window open. Other companies were going public successfully and he was getting positive feedback from the investment bankers that he kept in touch with that now might be the right time. It was a hard process, even with all the excitement around the company. "It's a unique investor that's willing to take that kind of risk in the public markets," Christoph observed. "I had to talk to a hundred and twenty people to get the fifteen institutions who really wanted in. But those fifteen institutions meant we would price successfully within our target range."

Even though Sirtris was still early in its development cycle, there was enough excitement around the company (and Christoph is very skilled at generating excitement) that he was able to successfully complete an IPO in May 2006, raising over $60 million in an IPO that opened at $10 per share and traded as high as $11 per share on the first day.

But there was no time to celebrate. He had a drug to deliver and a company to build. All the while, Christoph kept talking to the pharmaceutical companies. "My job is simply to maximize shareholder value," he explained. "So I kept in touch with all of these guys along the way. We wanted to only work with a company where the CEO and the head of R&D would commit to making this a major program. So a lot of our negotiations were around their investment in what we were doing for the next few years post-acquisition."

Christoph really didn't want to sell the company, and that sentiment probably allowed him to strike an even harder bargain with GSK. "We simply didn't want to sell. We wanted to keep progressing with the science and remain an independent public company." To make the deal work, he was able to convince GSK to commit to over $200 million in funding to Sirtris post-acquisition, on top of the $720 million that was paid out to the shareholders. This commitment sealed the deal for Christoph. Just as Eric Paley stayed at 3M after the sale of Brontes for two years to continue to see the original vision through, Christoph has stayed at GSK, serving on the R&D executive committee, which helps prioritize the company's investments.

The willingness to stick around after the exit, as both Eric and Christoph did, is an important barometer for VCs when assessing entrepreneurs. I remember making a reference call to a VC friend about a CEO I was backing. After giving me a very positive reference on the CEO with whom he had previously worked, my VC friend began to dwell on this CEO's inability to "see things through."

"What are you talking about?" I asked. "He completed the sale of the company and made you millions!"

"Yes," this VC retorted, "but he didn't stick around to see the escrow payment released."

The escrow is a portion of the acquisition proceeds, say 10 or 15 percent, that the acquirer holds back and places in a secure bank account for, say, twelve to eighteen months. It is set up to make sure there's nothing funny that comes up post-acquisition. If everything goes as it should after the acquisition and integration is complete, the escrow is released to the start-up's shareholders. If there are issues, the acquirer submits a claim against some or all of the escrowed funds.

My VC friend concluded, "I like my CEOs to be stewards for every last one of my investment dollars."

EXIT ONLY IF YOU ARE DONE

Exits are tricky, emotional—especially for the entrepreneur—and complicated for all parties.

Timing and your own personal commitment are both important factors. Twitter's Jack Dorsey gets asked the question every day—when will Twitter exit? He explained to me his views on this issue in a way that reinforces my thesis that the best entrepreneurs don't focus on the money, they focus on their passion and dream for the business.

"You always have to go back to the question, 'Is exiting the right thing for the product?'" Jack explained. "There were many times in our history when, technology-wise, we weren't up to snuff and we could have used more infrastructure. We could have used the resources of a Google or a Facebook or a Yahoo! But until you feel like you've completed some aspects of the vision, it just doesn't make sense to hand it over. If you have that idea and you've more or less seen the end of it, and now you're just racking your brain trying to figure out how to push it any further, the product might be better off in the hands of someone else, because you've done what you can. That's basically what it comes down to for me. Are you done? If you are, then exit. If you're not, keep going for it."

7

THE VENTURE-BACKED START-UP: AMERICA'S GREATEST EXPORT

American history is full of stories of great entrepreneurs who helped build the country and its position in the world. Ben Franklin—inventor, philosopher, statesman, and writer—was also a great entrepreneur who combined practical application with commercial instincts. Thomas Edison continued in this great tradition throughout the nineteenth century and, to this day, is the holder of more patents than any individual in U.S. history (although, now in the number two spot with over 750 and counting, MIT professor Bob Langer might someday surpass him). Modern iconic entrepreneurs, such as Bill Gates, Steve Jobs, Michael Dell, Jeff Bezos, and others, continue to inspire young entrepreneurs around the globe to pursue the art of the possible.

In the last few decades, the venture capital industry has worked to accelerate entrepreneurship and, as much as possible, improve the odds for success. By working with entrepreneurs in a range of industries across a number of business cycles, VCs try to figure out the formula for entrepreneurial success and impart those lessons to the next generation of would-be Franklins and Edisons. After decades spent perfecting the recipe and passing it on from generation to generation of VCs, they have begun to export it beyond America's shores. In the last ten years, VCs from Silicon Valley and Boston have jumped on airplanes and traveled throughout Europe, Asia, the Middle East, and beyond to instill their brand of entrepreneurship, sponsoring venture capital funds in these regions and exporting their company-building lessons and discipline. More recently, local VCs have taken root.

When one travels to some of these countries and talks to the VCs there, the conversations have a familiar ring. They could just as easily be taking place at a local watering hole in Silicon Valley or off Route 128. The VCs outside the United States operate by many of the same rules and with the same objectives. They, too, raise capital from limited partners, many of whom include or are similar to the major U.S. limited partners— the same endowments, the same pension funds. And they try to invest in great entrepreneurs, many of whom are educated in the United States, and seek exits in the form of IPOs (on the local stock exchange or, more attractive, a U.S.-based exchange such as the NASDAQ) or trade sales (often led by the global leaders, like Microsoft, IBM, HP, and Google).

As the economies in India, China, Southeast Asia, Eastern Europe, and other areas of the world grow and their infrastructures become more capable of supporting and sustaining their native markets, we will continue to see growth in the application of the VC-backed start-up model around the world. If you were a smart, ambitious, wired young person living in, say, Indonesia, why wouldn't you want to try to create the "eBay, Google, Amazon, Facebook of Indonesia." In fact, there are thousands of entrepreneurs right now trying to start such ventures in each of the major developed and developing countries. If these online businesses can be created in America without the need for equipment, heavy-duty science, or particular know-how, why not elsewhere? And if U.S.-trained or -influenced VCs are on hand to help out, all the better.

In the next few sections, I will profile some examples of the practitioners of the VC black art in China, Vietnam, and Europe and describe the rise of the VC business there. These profiles are not meant to be comprehensive. They are just a few samples of how the start-up business is being practiced abroad.

EXPLOSIVE GROWTH IN CHINA

China and India are two countries where venture capital has developed rapidly. China's venture capital industry has exploded, from nothing a decade ago to over $4 billion in 2010, with expectations that it will continue to grow rapidly in the next few years. India's story is a similar one at a more modest scale, with $1 billion in venture investments made in 2010. A closer look at the firms making these investments reveals American roots and training. Like their U.S. counterparts, many of the general partners were educated at elite universities and graduate programs in America. Many of the firms are led by executives who learned the art of venture capital in America, either as VCs themselves or as entrepreneurs at VC-backed companies. And an increasingly large number of these firms abroad are sponsored or partially owned by American VCs. Accel, Benchmark, DFJ, Kleiner Perkins, Sequoia Capital, and many other top-tier venture capital firms have established subsidiaries or joint ventures in Asia and Europe to export their brands in those geographies.

One interesting distinction between China and India is that the Chinese VC investments tend to be inwardly focused, pursuing opportunities within the domestic market. The Indian VC investments are more global in focus. A Stanford study that analyzed the market focus of Chinese and Indian VC-backed start-ups found that 73 percent of the Indian companies were internationally focused, while 87 percent of Chinese start-ups were domestically focused.[17] The magnitude and growth of the domestic market in China and the emerging middle class are the key drivers of this phenomenon.

An interesting case study in China is represented by Quan Zhou, managing director of IDG-Accel China. Quan began his venture capital career when he co-founded IDG Technology Venture Investment, Inc., a fund established in 1992 at the initiative of IDG chairman Pat McGovern as a way to recycle his profits from IDG's magazine businesses in China. Since its modest beginning with its $75 million first fund, the firm has become one of the leading venture capital firms in China. The firm has nearly $4 billion in capital under management across nine funds with more than two hundred

---

17. "Venture Capital in China and India—A Comparison" by Martin Kenney of Stanford University, 2002.

portfolio companies and thirty investment professionals in four offices.

Born in China, Quan came to the United States to earn his PhD in fiber optics at Rutgers University. Quan worked as an engineering consultant for several years and joined IDG in 1992. Pat McGovern, IDG's chairman and founder, and Hugo

Quan Zhou

Shong, IDG's Asia president, tapped Quan to start the first IDG Ventures China fund, initially in partnership with the Shanghai municipal government. Quan and McGovern went on to establish other government partnerships, replicating the partnership with other major municipalities such as Beijing and Guangdong because, he told me, "there was a lack of legal environment adaptable to VC investing."

Quan had no formal VC training and so had to learn on the job. McGovern smartly set up an advisory board for Quan and his partners, recruiting Stephen Coit, an experienced VC and former general partner from Charles River Ventures, a venerable Boston-based firm. As the Chinese market grew, with Stephen's help, Quan studied and followed the American VC model and developed his skills to become one of the preeminent VCs in China. One of the top Silicon Valley VC firms, Accel Partners, struck a deal with Quan and McGovern to have IDG Ventures China serve as the China-based manager of Accel's VC efforts, and the firm's name was changed to IDG-Accel China.

Quan and his partners have invested in such start-ups as Baidu, cTrip, and Dangdang, which were modeled after

Google, Expedia, and Amazon, respectively. Baidu, the native search engine company that is more popular than Google in China, had a very successful IPO in 2005 on the NASDAQ and, as of this writing, has a market capitalization of $50 billion. IDG Ventures China's investment in Baidu of a mere $1.5 million returned over $100 million to the fund at the time its stake was sold.

Baidu's founder, Robin Li, came to the United States as a student to get his master's degree in computer science at the State University of New York at Buffalo. From there, he worked for a few technology companies, including venture-backed Infoseek, an early Internet search engine start-up. Returning to China to found Baidu in January 2000, Li took back with him everything he learned from his time in the United States to build the dominant search engine in the country.

Another of Quan's investments is MySpace China, a joint venture between IDG-Accel China and Rupert Murdoch and News Corporation to replicate the success of the popular social networking site in China. During Quan's frequent visits to the United States, he periodically sits down with venture capitalists on both coasts and asks them the same simple question: "What's hot?" He takes this knowledge home with him and matches great local entrepreneurs with proven U.S. business models to build valuable companies customized for China.

When I asked him to compare the VC industry in China to that of the United States, Quan told me that the approach and attitude are surprisingly similar. "The language is different, but the mentality, the attitude, and the thinking process are really similar. We're all just human beings—people talking about how to build a business in China, just like they do in

United States. For the venture capitalist, we practice and we learn from the U.S. and then we excel. So, on the surface there are lots of differences, but down deep things are the same."

The first big wave of entrepreneurial activity in China came in the late 1990s, with the rise of Internet commerce. "Investors before that time weren't really serious," Quan said. "Then firms like us really started making money. Then there were many, many venture capitalists that jumped into China. And for a while, there was a lot of money around."

But the meaning of "a lot of money" is relative. The early investments in Chinese businesses were relatively small. "In the 1990s, we were doing hundred-thousand-dollar and two-hundred-thousand-dollar deals," Quan remembers. "The strategy was just go with the market and watch it grow. Even so, many early investors lost a lot of money, partly because the start-up infrastructure was not there yet."

Because the corporate IT industry is at the primordial soup stage in China, the major focus of investment is currently in the consumer sector. As Quan told me, there are many industries that are underpopulated by private companies and dominated by state-owned entities. "There are no publishing companies, no big media companies. There are no big travel agencies. All are state-owned, and slow." These industrial gaps present numerous entrepreneurial opportunities.

Although many of the companies Quan and his VC counterparts invest in look similar to the kind of investments venture capitalists pursue in the United States, many look very different. One of the firm's most successful investments was in Home Inn, a chain of budget hotels. Imagine DFJ's Tim Draper, with his aversion to investing in laundromats, receiving the pitch for a budget hotel chain start-up in the United States. Quan's firm's investment in Home Inn led to a return of more than fifty times when Home Inn went public in 2006 on the NASDAQ. As of this writing, the company's market capitalization is over $1 billion. One of the reasons for the different opportunities is that the Chinese economy is growing so quickly (GDP grew on average 10 percent annually throughout the first decade in the twenty-first century) that even traditional industries provide very large, fast-growing investment opportunities.

There are now so many aspiring entrepreneurs in China that Quan needs to do very little prospecting. Some 2,000–3,000 business plans come to him each year, and he and his partners review most of them themselves. He can dispense with the majority of them within five minutes—Quan's firm funds only fifteen to twenty companies a year.

The excitement about starting businesses in China has reached the point that Quan and his team have become celebrities in the country. Would-be entrepreneurs frequently walk in off the street and, like paparazzi, line up at Quan's office door. But rather than snapping photographs or seeking interviews, these hangers-on are hoping to catch Quan for a two-minute pitch (the elevator pitch, literally) and walk out with a commitment. Entrepreneurship has become so popular in China that a television show was created and Quan's partner, Hugo Shong, appears on the show weekly to listen to aspiring entrepreneurs pitch their business plans and provides feedback. Presumably, the show only becomes the kind of soap opera I described in Chapter 5 after the financing.

VIEWPOINT FROM VIETNAM

It's not terribly surprising that China, with its rapidly developing economy, huge population, and focus on business, has seen such a surge of start-ups. But China is hardly the only country that has been bitten by the entrepreneurial bug. Vietnam's Henry Nguyen, the managing general director at IDG Ventures Vietnam, is another example of how the American brand of entrepreneurism can be exported and adapted to other local needs and conditions.

Henry Nguyen

Born in Vietnam, Henry was airlifted out of Saigon in 1975 when he was not yet two, and spent his childhood and youth in America. He earned a BA in classics from Harvard College, followed by an MBA from Kellogg School of Management and an MD from Northwestern University Medical School. While an undergraduate, he co-founded S2S Medical Publishing—eventually acquired by Blackwell Science—and Medschool.com, which received $25 million in VC funding. Henry had planned to become a surgeon or investment banker but wound up running the largest venture capital fund in Vietnam in 2005, at the ripe old age of thirty. Known as the "John Doerr of Vietnam," Henry has been so instrumental in creating a VC-backed start-up culture in Vietnam that he even invented the Vietnamese phrase for venture capital (literally translated into "risk growth capital"). Henry hopes to emulate

Quan Zhou's success and make Vietnam into the "next China." Just as Quan did throughout the 1990s, he's placing bets on who will be the first to start an Amazon, eBay, or Google in Vietnam.

Bubbling with enthusiasm, Henry told me about how he came to be the go-to VC in Vietnam when he was still in his early thirties. "I was born in Vietnam in 1973," he said. "My dad was a civil engineer and managed a lot of big projects around Danang and Hue. We had friends in the U.S. embassy and when the end of the war was near, they helped us get out. We were very fortunate to be able to leave when we did. We emigrated through the Philippines and settled outside Washington, D.C., where I grew up. I sometimes joke that, if I didn't look in the mirror, I would have thought I was a typical American suburban kid."

Many factors pushed Henry toward a career outside the mainstream. First, he strongly felt the American entrepreneurial influence. "Growing up in American society, there are so many Horatio Alger stories, self-made men types, that you think anything is possible." At the same time, Henry felt what he calls Asian "filiopiety"—a great, even excessive, reverence toward one's ancestors—that created an enormous drive to "kick ass in school and be at the top of my class to make my parents proud of me."

His position as the youngest child in the family also played a role. "When you're the youngest, you can go one of two ways. You can be ultraconservative and live in this comfortable nest that the social support system provides you. Part of my life was living in that shell. But the rebellious part, the rule breaker part, was, 'Wow, you know what? I can break a lot of rules and

I have a support system that'll catch me if I fall. I'm going to try to do a lot of wild, crazy things.'"

For Henry, wild and crazy meant starting businesses at a young age. "I once read that what you're doing at ten defines your passion in life. In 1981, the IBM PC came out. My family, a good middle-class immigrant family but not really well off, shelled out the $3,000 to buy one. I fell in love with computers and technology. Having that IBM PC turned me into a young hacker, dialing into county school computers and local bulletin boards."

An interest in buying more computer gear led Henry to start his first business together with a friend. "With an old dot-matrix printer, we created a printing business making listing sheets for Realtors in the area. My friend's mom was a Realtor and, in the beginning, I think she saw us as a charity case, paying us to stay out of trouble. As long as we were in the basement on the computer, we weren't potentially doing greater harm. She paid us ten dollars for every listing sheet we created. And to us, that was fantastic."

Eventually, Henry and his friend were doing cover-sheet printing for all the brokers in the office and then built a network of Realtor clients throughout the neighborhood. They bought more computers and more equipment. "That was a seminal experience that got us on the road to being entrepreneurs."

In college, as a premed, Henry expanded his business activities. He hooked up with three friends to start a publishing company. "We were taking organic chemistry and physics to prepare for the MCATs [Medical College Admissions Test]. I had all these notes, and so did my friends. I thought I might as well put all the information together and that it would be better than the Kaplan test prep books. It would be the student-to-student skinny."

Over the next four years—from sophomore year at Harvard to his second year of medical school at Northwestern—Henry and his friends built the company into a substantial business, eventually publishing thirty-six different titles and selling a total of some 350,000 copies. That was sufficient volume to catch the attention of a U.K. science publisher, Blackwell Science, who bought the company for $5 million. "We said, 'Man, look at all this money we made! What are we going to do with it?' I did the stupid thing and bought a car, but then rolled two-thirds of the money into another start-up."

Throughout his childhood and into college, Henry had always thought of himself as a "warm-blooded American suburban kid" with virtually no ties to his native Vietnam. "I'm a little ashamed to say it, but I grew up almost denying my heritage of being Vietnamese. I was proud to be American." But, after graduating from Harvard, Henry took a job with Let's Go Travel Guides. His goal was to get one of the plum assignments, preferably rewriting the Rome guide. "You live in Rome for ten weeks and your job is to eat and party every day. You can't beat it." But the publisher was planning a guidebook for Southeast Asia and needed someone to write the Vietnam section. "So they went down the roster of staff writers and said, 'Oh, this guy's got a Vietnamese last name, ask him.' And I remember laughing and telling my editor, 'You might as well pick the name Smith because he's probably just as Vietnamese as I am.'"

Eventually, Henry was talked into doing the job and, in the summer of 1995, off he went to Vietnam. "That trip was a revelation," he told me. "It was like, 'Oh, my God. Vietnam is a really cool place. It isn't *Platoon* or *Apocalypse Now.*' Maybe it was as simple as the food, the language, and things like that. Maybe it was meeting my father's side of the family that I'd never met, including my grandmother. Although it was all completely new to me, it felt like home. That summer, I fell in love with Vietnam."

The experience of that summer stuck with him. After earning his MBA and MD simultaneously from Northwestern in 2001, Henry decided not to practice medicine but instead pursued his business interests and took an offer in investment banking with Goldman Sachs in New York. He got an apartment in the city and was ready to go to work. But then Henry's father asked him to help out with a telecommunications company he was starting in Vietnam, and Henry deferred the Goldman Sachs position. "I thought it would be a short-term stint in Vietnam and, when summer was over, I would go back to the real job in New York. But at the end of the summer, I flew back to the U.S. and talked to the recruiting partner and said, 'What if I told you that I had some things to work on for the next six months in Vietnam and I'll start at the beginning of next year instead.' He said, 'Fine. Call me at the beginning of the year.'"

Henry flew out of New York on September 9, 2001, and landed in Vietnam the evening of September 11 as the attack on the World Trade Center swept the news. "I flipped on CNN and thought, 'What the hell just happened while I was on the plane?' Everybody was in shock. I remember I was in my hotel in Hanoi thinking, 'This must be a little bit of fate. I can't imagine a better or safer place I could be than in Vietnam right now.'"

Henry stayed on in Vietnam, but checked in with Goldman Sachs periodically. "Before I knew it, two years had gone by. And at the end of those two years, I had completed my love affair with Vietnam." He informed the Goldman Sachs partner that he would not be taking the job after all.

Over the next three years, Henry helped build the family's telecommunications business from nothing to a $30 million enterprise. Then, he had the opportunity to switch over to the VC side and start a $50 million VC fund in Vietnam, launching it in 2005 with IDG's backing. "I find being on the venture side of things extremely rewarding because you get to be around revolutionary stuff that's going on. You get to test your mettle as a futurist. On top of that, I get to do a job that should be a social and economic game changer here. We're bringing a formal venture culture and ecosystem to Vietnam. We're changing the way businesses get started and the way private enterprise has access to resources like capital, expertise, and human resources. It's kind of like getting to be Sequoia in Silicon Valley back in the seventies. That's what it feels like to be in Vietnam today."

Henry's training as a venture capitalist over the years has been both from his on-the-ground experience and mentorship and connections. China's Quan Zhou has served as a great role model for Henry, as have Stephen Coit of Charles River Ventures and my partner Michael Greeley. They have coached Henry on venture capital as practiced in China and the United States, allowing Henry to adapt the model to Vietnam.

Henry told me that the entrepreneurial energy in Vietnam right now is palpable. "You step off the plane and you feel, 'Good Lord, where is all this commercial and entrepreneurial energy coming from?' It's jarring because you don't expect it. It literally spills out into the streets. Everybody's building something or trying to buy or sell something. They're hustling, scheming to figure out what's the next great opportunity."

Even with all that commercial energy, the environment in Vietnam is not necessarily easy for VCs to negotiate successfully, especially for those without experience in the culture. "This is fertile ground to be a rule breaker, in the sense that everything's ambiguous," Henry told me. "What we're dealing with here is very primal. It's jungle law. It's more of a street fight than anywhere else."

So selecting the right businesses and the right entrepreneurs to back in Vietnam can be even trickier than in other markets. Henry tends to favor Vietnamese nationals who intuitively understand the market. Even better if they have been educated abroad or worked abroad for a multinational or even worked for a multinational in Vietnam. Whatever their background, Henry spends a good deal of time educating the entrepreneurs with whom he works. "We take entrepreneurs through VC 101. Negotiating a term sheet, liquidation preferences, redemption, all the covenants."

Many of the businesses start up with tiny investments—a few thousand dollars, twenty thousand, a few hundred thousand—but the amounts of money are still huge by local standards. "When we write them a check—even a modest one of a couple hundred thousand dollars—that's more than any of these businesses have ever had to manage."

The amount of money looks so large to most Vietnamese entrepreneurs that many of them think of it not as an investment, but as the exit. "They think, 'Now I can start paying my relatives!' So we have to put in all these covenants that, in the U.S., people would be aghast at. They'd see them as micromanaging. We require bank statements monthly so we know that the money didn't just disappear and that bad things are not happening. It's a lot of education, a lot of hand-holding. We have to make them understand that they shouldn't try to slip a little bit of money out here or there. We say, 'We understand you need to make a living. But realize the end game is this. If you do the right things, you're going to be a millionaire. Imagine that!'"

When Henry Nguyen started in Vietnam, there was no word or phrase that described venture capital, so he had to develop one. "The term we chose translates directly to 'risk growth capital.' We wanted to make the point that we're not risk takers. We're not guys who are jumping out of airplanes. It's a risk because, hey, these are very young businesses that are trying to do novel things and the odds of success are against them. Secondly, we wanted to say that capital is for growth. Using the word 'risk,' by itself, puts a vision of gambling into people's heads. So we were trying to express something thoughtful— there's high risk, but we're trying to grow businesses to be big businesses."

THE EXPLOSION OF VINAGAMES

One of Henry's first investments was in an online gaming start-up called VinaGames (the word "Vina" means "Vietnam" in Vietnamese). "Gaming was number two on our hit list," he explained to me. Henry cooked up the idea together with one of his entrepreneurs in residence, Bryan Pelz, and seeded the company with a $300,000 investment in May 2005 to see if he could create the company. "We brought in an American serial entrepreneur [Bryan] and connected him with one of our old colleagues who was a telecom engineer and knows the Internet backbone of Vietnam top to bottom." Henry added to the team three young Vietnamese game players. "They're passionate about games and totally understand the market. But they're a little green. So I figured, why don't I mash them all together?"

This mix of American entrepreneurship with Vietnamese know-how and passionate domain experience proved to be a great kickoff for the company. With the business plan developed and the team built, Henry and Bryan saw an opportunity to kick-start the company by merging it with an existing gaming operator, and so some more capital went in. With these humble beginnings, the company exploded on the gaming scene in Vietnam. Since its initial launch in the fall of 2005, VinaGames has grown rapidly with 14 million users—nearly half of all Vietnamese households! Not even four years old, the company has grown from those five founders to over a thousand employees. And the business model is working, with tens of millions of dollars in annual profits. If the company continues to grow and progress, it could be the first billion-dollar IPO out of Vietnam, thanks to Henry's shrewd "mashing together."

Henry sees enormous potential in the Internet and online ventures in Vietnam, for two reasons. "First, Vietnam is an incredibly young market. The average age of the population is probably twenty-four. Second, Vietnam is literate. We have a ninety-six percent literacy rate. Pretty much everybody gets educated up through eighth grade. In essence, Vietnam is as young as India and as literate as China. And then, of course, you have a decent market size. Eighty-six million people now and growing. Vietnam will be one hundred million people within the next eight or nine years. Add to that the number of Internet users. When we started in 2004, there were over three million Internet users in Vietnam, according to government statistics. At the end of 2007, there were close to twenty-two million Internet users. That's a sixfold growth in users in the last four years."

Henry's path to becoming a VC in Vietnam reflects many of my own experiences—a little serendipity had more impact than any master plan. He observed, "When I talk to university students here in Vietnam, or wherever, I tell them that being a venture capitalist is not a career you usually think about as a kid. You don't say, 'Man, I want to grow up and be a VC.' You don't even know what it is. I didn't. I was following the footsteps of my siblings to be a doctor. I was close to graduating medical school before I realized that I'm more a goose than a duck. I wasn't going to be a doctor. It isn't what I was made to be. I was made to be an entrepreneur."

SUBTLE DIFFERENCES IN EUROPE

In Europe, the VC game is played in much the same way as it is in the rest of the world. Europeans have long been entrepreneurs and venture capitalists and, of course, funded and organized many of the voyages of discovery and settlement—starting in

the fifteenth and sixteenth centuries—that led to the establish-
ment of colonies in the New World.

In modern times, Europe's VC industry is a fraction of the
size it is in the United States, but still substantial. In 2010,
European VCs invested $5 billion. Unlike China and India,
where VC investment is growing rapidly, VC investment in
Europe has been relatively stagnant over the last few years and
is not projected to grow in the next few years. Many blame the
cultural barriers to entrepreneurship in Europe, where there is
less comfort and tolerance with failure and risk taking.

Irena Goldenberg is one of the very few women in the venture capital industry and one of the *very*, very few female VCs
in Europe. Born in Ukraine, she came to the United States as
a teenager, attended MIT, and then worked for the consulting
firm Bain & Company. We hired her as an associate at Flybridge Capital Partners before she returned to school to earn
her MBA from Harvard Business School. While at HBS, she
spent a summer at Index Venture, a European venture firm, and
gained exposure to European markets and VCs. She decided she
wanted to stay in Europe after graduation and is now a principal with the European arm of Highland Capital Partners, oper-

Irena Goldenberg

ating out of Geneva, Switzerland.

When I asked Irena about practicing venture capital in Europe and how
she sources her deals, she reflected that
the techniques are quite similar to her
experience in the United States. When
she first arrived in Europe, Irena had
to build out her network, as all VCs
do. "There was a lot of cold calling,

cold emailing, and working the alumni network—HBS, Bain, and MIT. By seeking out deals, you create a virtuous cycle such that you end up having more and more deals come your way. So there's not a ton of difference in that process, to the extent that you are a proactive VC. You apply a similar methodology, you seek out deals on a pan-European basis, and that works."

There are important differences between the American and European venture capital industries, however, starting with the size and number of funds. "There are really just a handful of sizable venture funds actively operating in Europe. So one positive aspect of the industry, at least from a venture perspective, is that there's not as much competition for hot deals as there would be in Boston or in the Valley."

There are cultural differences across European countries. "Europe is certainly not a single geography," Irena said, "and can't really be treated as such. Cross-country nuances emerge in types of teams, deals, technologies, expectations of entrepreneurs, and expectations of core investors—these vary quite a bit by geography. In the U.S., in terms of target markets, VCs don't think, 'Hey, I'm going to dominate Texas, and then maybe I'll enter California.' But this is very much the case in Europe."

Entrepreneurs in less populous European countries have a different attitude than their counterparts in larger geographies because their domestic market is so small. "Entrepreneurs in the smaller European countries—such as Sweden, Finland, Estonia, Denmark—often think bigger," Irena explains. "A Swedish entrepreneur, for example, sees the world as his target market. He does not build to the Swedish market; he is building to the world. French, British, and German entrepreneurs, on the other hand, are often building to their own domestic markets, which in their mind, are, of course, the largest markets in Europe. But to us, it is often not a global enough vision."

As a result of this global perspective, entrepreneurial talent is dispersed in Europe. "We look for top-quality management with global ambition," Irena said, "which involves getting on a plane every week in search of the best entrepreneurs in Barcelona, Berlin, Stockholm, or elsewhere. There is no Silicon Valley equivalent in Europe. With the emergence of Eastern Europe, there's a new pool of highly educated, first-time entrepreneurs from Bulgaria to Slovenia to Russia that are eager for success."

One example of the impact Eastern Europe is having on entrepreneurial innovation is at LogMeIn, a software company started in Budapest, Hungary. The company's CEO moved to the United States, established sales and marketing headquarters, raised venture capital, and successfully took the company public in 2007, all while maintaining its development center in Budapest.

There are differences, too, in the experience and number of entrepreneurs in Europe. "There's an emerging class of entrepreneurs that everyone in the venture community wants to be best friends with," Irena told me. "These are very experienced entrepreneurial managers—meaning second- and third-time entrepreneurs, who have built companies, exited them, and are doing it again. But there just aren't enough of those investments to go around. And that, too, is a big difference from the U.S."

European entrepreneurs, even the experienced ones, have a different style than those in the United States, Irena says. "They are much more prone to telling you the truth about everything—all of the darkest, deepest secrets and risks. They are less polished salesmen. They are hesitant about putting together a plan that they think may be unachievable. So you have to push them on accelerating their vision. Or they might have a big vision but the timeline is too long. I think the American perspective is more optimistic, often over-optimistic, about compressing timelines and moving faster."

European VCs and entrepreneurs also have a different approach to some of the social norms around due diligence. "The one thing I must say about doing business in Europe," Irena said, "is that the default small talk is very different. No discussions about baseball or American football. When we did our deep diligence process with a German company, for example, they invited us to fly in the day before, go to the opera in the evening with them, and then spend the following day together drilling down on business fundamentals. This is something that would never happen in the U.S."

Irena had one experience that I would be hard-pressed to judge as more European or American in nature. "I had a meeting in Spain when we were attempting to close a deal with my senior partner, the management team, and me. At the end of the meeting, we asked if they had any remaining questions about us, about our process, about the way we work, or if we could provide references. The only question that came back was, and I quote, 'Irena, are you married?' We almost fell off the chairs laughing."

The growth of venture capital outside the United States is a very positive by-product of the flattening of the world. As the start-up ecosystems mature in these countries, more opportunities will be available for entrepreneurs to get access to capital and good company-building advice. One can only hope that the innovations that are developed outside the United States will find their way here eventually.

LOOKING AHEAD

Increasing globalism is sure to characterize the world of start-ups in the next decade or more, but what else does the future hold for this small but very influential industry? Despite a period of economic uncertainty, the entrepreneurs and VCs with whom I spoke are by and large, not surprisingly, bullish on the role of the start-up.

"This is the best time to be an entrepreneur," gushed DFJ's Tim Draper when I asked for his views of the current economic environment. "This is the best time for entrepreneurs to turn the whole thing on its ear because there's total confusion. Existing companies are reeling, smart people are out of a job, and new technologies are going to change the way we work and play. Entrepreneurs are heroes and they will figure out ways to reinvent, time and time again."

The data support Tim's bullish outlook. The venture capital business has survived and thrived through numerous boom and bust cycles, and great companies have been built at every step of the way. The PC revolution and the boom of the mid- and late 1970s led to the founding and VC funding of important companies like Microsoft (1975) and Apple (1977). These heady times led to strong returns for venture capital funds, with average investment returns of 15–20 percent per year for the average-performing venture fund, never mind the top-tier funds.[18]

But the boom times were followed by a bust cycle in the early 1980s. The combination of the recession and overfunded sectors (at one point, there were forty-three different disk drive manufacturers funded by venture capitalists) led to a plummeting of venture capital returns.[19] VC funds raised and deployed in the early 1980s returned a modest 5–10 percent per year, and many bemoaned the death of the industry. Despite these woes, during that bust cycle, entrepreneurs founded and VCs funded some extraordinary companies: Sun (1982), Compaq (1982), and Cisco (1984), to name a few. When the economy recovered in the late 1980s, these companies were well positioned to go public, as Cisco did successfully in 1990.

The boom and bust cycle continued during the 1990s, with the venture capital industry growing slowly from $4-5 billion per year in the 1980s to $5–10 billion in the first half of the 1990s. The Internet revolution resulted in an explosion in entrepreneurship, and the amount of venture capital investment in start-ups climbed from $10 billion in 1996 to nearly $100 billion in 2000. Average fund returns exploded to 30–50

---

18. Venture Economics and retired CRV general partner Ted Dintersmith, who developed an influential presentation in 2003 from which I have drawn out many of these themes and content for this section.

19. NVCA 2001 Yearbook.

percent per year during the first half of the 1990s and climbed even from there as the IPO market seemed to accept companies on concepts alone. For example, Pets.com, an online community for pet lovers, went public in February 2000. The IPO resulted in a $300 million valuation. The only problem was that the company had negligible revenue and no sustainable business model. It went out of business in November 2000, less than a year later.

Since the Internet bubble burst, the VC industry has rationalized. But many argue that it hasn't rationalized enough. The annual U.S. funding level settled in at $25–30 billion per year in 2002–2008, climbing slightly just as the economic head winds began. With the economic shakeout of 2008–2009 and a slow IPO market, I predict these numbers will fall to $15–20 billion in the coming years. The industry is still very young, only forty years old, but is arguably beginning to mature and settle. Even with $15–20 billion invested each year, it is a stretch to describe the industry as one in which every investor should participate. "Venture capital is simply not an asset class," Brad Feld of Foundry Group insists. "It's a niche category. But a niche category with tremendous leverage."

Still, $15–20 billion of venture capital outlay a year means thousands of potentially great companies will be started and funded each year, and many people join Tim Draper in arguing that downturns can be the best time to create new companies. Howard Morgan of First Round Capital put it simply: "This country was built on entrepreneurship. It's during tough times like this, when a whole bunch of talented people are thrown out of work, that you get folks sitting at home thinking creatively, 'What can I do?'"

I talked with Terry McGuire, chairman of the National Venture Capital Association (NVCA) and co-founder of Polaris Venture Partners, to get his take on the state of the industry. Polaris is a multistage firm that focuses on IT and life science start-ups, with offices in Boston and Seattle. After earning his master's in engineering from Dartmouth College, McGuire worked at a software start-up, then began his MBA program at Harvard. He joined a VC firm after business school in 1982 and later worked at Burr, Egan, Deleage & Co., before he left to co-found Polaris with John Flint and Steve Arnold in 1994. Terry has served on the boards of multiple successful start-ups, including Cubist Pharmaceuticals, Akamai Technologies, and deCODE Genetics. He also has a long-standing collaborative partnership with prolific inventor Professor Bob Langer of MIT, having funded fifteen of the twenty-five companies Bob has helped start.

Terry McGuire

Terry's investment in Akamai may be one of the most successful venture capital investments in history. Founded by MIT professor Tom Leighton and his graduate student Daniel Lewin, Akamai raised an $8 million Series A round of capital in 1998 from Polaris and Battery and then participated in a $20 million Series B round a few months later. In November 1999, just fourteen months later, the company went public and reached a peak market capitalization of over $20 billion. Trust me when I say the investors did very, very well. As of early 2010, Akamai had approximately $1 billion in sales, a market capitalization of $6 billion, and is the dominant player in delivering content across the Internet around the globe.

Given his broad experience and his position as chair of the NVCA, Terry has thought a lot about the ups and downs of entrepreneurship and its long-term prospects. "The last ten years, from 1998 to 2008, have been marked by pretty severe swings. In the 1998–1999 bubble it looked like you were printing money. For those of us who had been in the business for a while, it was a little confusing. Are people really paying that kind of money for this kind of business? And yet there were some good companies there. Then the bubble burst, followed by a period of relative stability, but not a ton of traction. In late 2008 and 2009, the economy suffered a major economic meltdown. So it has been a funky decade. But it's important that people take a long-term perspective. I think that fundamentally, as an industry, it will remain very healthy."

Terry thinks that the number of IPOs—which was a pitifully small number in the second half of 2008 and in 2009—will increase in 2010 and 2011. "But start-ups are going to have a much higher threshold to prove that an IPO is the right way to go. We can look at companies that are growing very nicely, that are profitable, that don't need financial markets, and those are companies that will be very appropriate IPO candidates—at the right moment. But the heady days of 1999, when companies got started and six weeks later were valued at a billion dollars, and then nine months after that tried to go public, are gone."

And, frankly, that's good for everyone. Quick riches and unrealistic valuations are not, and should never be, the goal of a serious start-up. VCs are attracted to entrepreneurs whose business models transcend economic cycles rather than those who are interested in the "quick flip" by selling their start-up after a year or two. It takes time to build robust, scalable products and successful distribution channels, and for management teams to gel into a cohesive operating unit. Serious entrepreneurs and VCs recognize this and will continue to adjust their operating assumptions to factor this additional time element into their projections. It will mean lower rates of return for limited partners, as time is the enemy of all illiquid investments. But it should result in creating more sustainable, valuable, and important companies at the end of the development cycle.

Venture-backed start-ups have something magic about them. Whether it's because of the discipline that an outside investor imposes on a start-up, the value and experience that VCs bring to the table, or simply a selection bias, venture-backed start-ups outperform all other forms of entrepreneurial ventures. "With forty or fifty years of venture capital investing, why are these companies still growing jobs at twice the rate of the other members of the private sector?" asks Polaris's McGuire. "You have to go back to the core. We back great people. Combine that with smart, patient, and experienced capital. When you put those two forces together, you have this enormous engine for growth. If you really look at the impact we've had as an industry, it's been enormous."

The NVCA compiled some telling statistics on the impact the VC industry has had on the U.S. economy. Eighteen percent of U.S. GDP is generated by venture-backed companies. Ten percent of jobs and nearly 50 percent of all job growth comes from venture-backed companies. One in three Americans receives care from drugs that have come from venture-backed companies. This highly leveraged formula for success over the last forty years since General Doriot invested in Digital Equipment Computer remains strong.

LinkedIn's Reid Hoffman agrees that the VC-entrepreneur partnership will continue to play an important role in our society. "Everyone is some version of an entrepreneur now. The purest version—the one in which I create a new product, company, or service, and it's a whole new entity—will still be a limited percentage of people. But if you look at the world becoming flat and the accelerating time frames and increased competition, that's why everyone is focusing on innovation."

In a flatter world and with a larger population of innovators, the VC industry will need to transform itself. The old model of an exclusive club with opaque processes and secretive rules will no longer be effective. In the new model, which many of the VCs interviewed in this book are beginning to practice, the role of the VC is as a service provider to the entrepreneur. As such, VCs are becoming more transparent, open, and dynamic. Social media tools like Hoffman's LinkedIn and Dorsey's Twitter, as well as the forces of globalization, are enhancing the accessibility of the VC model and VCs themselves to entrepreneurs around the world.

At the same time that the VC industry is becoming more accessible, innovation is flourishing. MIT's Bob Langer observes that the research culture at universities and laboratories has changed. "Ten years ago, a lot of places in academia might not have wanted to create companies based on research innovations, but now it's more and more accepted. I've been doing this for twenty-five years, and certainly it wasn't respected when we started out. But today, throughout academia, starting companies is considered a positive thing to do."

Bob's lab at MIT, the Langer Lab, is teeming with interesting innovation and new scientific breakthroughs. When I asked Bob what drives him and his students, his answer was consistent with the comments by other entrepreneurs interviewed in this book. "To do more good," he replied immediately. "Of course we all want to make money, but money isn't the driver. Having an impact is the driver. Wherever I am in my life, I want to be doing things that I feel will have the greatest impact."

Ultimately, the desire to have an impact on the world and the passion for innovation is what makes this magic formula between entrepreneur and venture capitalist such a special one. The business and technology challenges of the twenty-first century are as fundamental as any that mankind has faced in its history. Harnessing renewable energy sources, accelerating medical advances while ensuring affordable health care, rolling out broadband wireless communications to the planet's billions of consumers who are coming online—these and many other global challenges will be faced with the same zeal that spurred the founders and venture capitalists profiled in this book.

With the right vision, passion, innovation, and a little capital sprinkled in, entrepreneurship spurred by venture capital is alive and well, with a bright future ahead of it. The world will be a better place because of it.

ACKNOWLEDGMENTS

It is hard to describe my appreciation for all who helped me with this ambitious project. Writing a book about venture capital and entrepreneurship while serving as a (more than) full-time venture capitalist required the patience and support of my partners (David Aronoff, Michael Greeley, Chip Hazard, and Jon Karlen), who have taught me so much about this business and make it fun every day. I also could never have undertaken this task without the help from my friends at the Butman Company, particularly John Butman and Anna Weiss. John was an invaluable guide and collaborator for me, a first-time author, throughout the entire process.

Others who I'm indebted to include my agent Todd Shuster at Zachary Shuster Harmsworth, and the folks at Penguin, particularly my skilled editor, Adrienne Schultz, as well as Adrian Zackheim and Brooke Carey.

I am, of course, greatly indebted to all who allowed me to interview them and include their wisdom, insights, and case studies in the book. Their stories really make the book. All of the entrepreneurs I have invested with and worked with also deserve my thanks for teaching me about the start-up game and giving me the real-life case studies and experience, over our many years working together, that I drew from in writing this book.

In addition to my partners, other Flybridge Capital Partners colleagues (Kate Castle, Robin Lockwood, Bruce Revzin, Matt Witheiler, and my dedicated and very competent assistant, Anna Dimaria), editors, and interviewees, I received wonderfully detailed feedback from numerous reviewers and supporters. Woody Benson, Joe Chernov, Fred Destin, Andy Doctoroff, Gary Eichhorn, Brad Feld, Rob Go, Brian Halligan, Ben Kaplan, my brother-in-law Bill Landay, Jason Mendelson, Andy Payne, Jessica Rosenbloom, Peter Russo, Dharmesh Shah, Noam Wasserman, Yifan Zhang, Ed Zimmerman, and each of the members of my Chavurah (Hallagans, Rock-Levys, and Sisenwines) particularly stand out, among many. I was also very fortunate to have parents who doubled as editors—supportive, yet discerning, of every word, concept, and point and willing to dedicate the time to review draft after draft.

Finally, my wife, Lynda Doctoroff Bussgang, has been incredibly supportive, patient, and tolerant of me throughout the process. I am fortunate to have had her as my life partner since that first day we met freshman year.

BLOG ROLL

There are many online resources for entrepreneurs and I have been grateful, in particular, for the insightful blogging from a number of VCs and entrepreneurs, many of whose materials have influenced and inspired the book. Here is a sampling.

David Aronoff (Twitter: @DBA)
Diary of a Geek VC
www.geekvc.com

Scott Austin (@ScottMAustin)
WSJ Venture Capital Dispatch
www.blogs.wsj.com/venturecapital

Henry Blodgett (@HBlodgett)
Business Insider
www.businessinsider.com

Jason Calacanis(@Jason Calacanis)
The Jason Calacanis Weblog
www.calacanis.com

Larry Cheng (@LarryVC)
Thinking About Thinking
www.larrycheng.com

Jeff Clavier (@JeffClavier)
Software Only
www.blog.softtechvc.com

David Cowan
(@YoungProfessor)
Who Has Time for This?
www.whohastimeforthis
.blogspot.com

Mark Peter Davis
(@MarkPeterDavis)
Venture Made Transparent
www.markpeterdavis.com

Fred Destin (@FDestin)
Open Source Venture Capital
www.freddestin.com

Chris Dixon (@CDixon)
Chris Dixon's Blog
www.cdixon.org

Don Dodge (@DonDodge)
Don Dodge on the Next Big
Thing
www.dondodge.typepad.com

Tim Draper (@TimDraper)
The Riskmaster
www.theriskmaster.blogspot.
com

Roger Ehrenberg
(@InfoArbitrage)
Info Arbitrage
www.InformationArbitrage.com

Brad Feld (@BFeld)
Feld Thoughts
www.feld.com

Seth Godin (@SethGodin)
Seth's Blog
www.sethgodin.typepad.com

Paul Graham (@PaulG)
www.paulgraham.com

Michael Greeley (@greels1)
On the Flying Bridge
www.ontheflyingbridge.word
press.com

Bill Gurley (@BGurley)
Above the Crowd
www.abovethecrowd.com

Chip Hazard (@CHazard)
Hazard Lights
www.hazardlights.net

Mike Hirshland (@VCMike)
VCMike's Blog
www.vcmike.wordpress.com

David Hornik
(@DavidHornik)
VentureBlog
www.ventureblog.com

Jeff Jarvis (@JeffJarvis)
BuzzMachine
www.buzzmachine.com

Jon Karlen (@JEKTweet)
Venturing Forth
www.venturingforth.typepad
.com

Guy Kawasaki
(@GuyKawasaki)
How to Change the World
www.blog.guykawasaki.com

Scott Kirsner
(@ScottKirsner)
Innovation Economy
www.boston.com/business/
technology/innoeco/

Josh Kopelman (@JoshK)
Redeye VC
www.redeye.firstround.com

Om Malik (@Om)
GigaOM
www.gigaom.com

Jonathan Marino (@JonMarino)
PE Hub
www.PeHub.com

Howard Morgan
(@HLMorgan)
WayTooEarly
www.waytooearly.firstround.
com

Jeff Nolan (@JeffNolan)
Venture Chronicles
www.jeffnolan.com/wp

Charlie O'Donnell
(@CEONYC)
This is going to be BIG
www.thisisgoingtobebig.com

Tim O'Reilly (@TimOReilly)
O'Reilly Radar
www.radar.oreilly.com/tim

Mark Pincus (@MarkPinc)
Mark Pincus Blog
www.markpincus.typepad
.com

Dan Primack (@DanPrimack)
Fortune
www.finance.fortune.cnn
.com

Naval Ravikant (@Naval) and
Babak Nivi (@Nivi)
Venture Hacks
www.venturehacks.com

Eric Ries (@EricRies)
Lessons Learned
www.startuplessonslearned
.com

Bijan Sabet (@Bijan)
Bijansabet.com
www.bijansabet.com

David Meerman Scott
(@DMScott)
Web Ink Now
www.webinknow.com

Dharmesh Shah (@Dharmesh)
OnStartups
www.onstartups.com

Ed Sim (@EdSim)
BeyondVC
www.beyondvc.com

David Skok (@BostonVC)
For Entrepreneurs
www.forentrepreneurs.com

Mark Suster (@MSuster)
Both Sides of the Table
www.bothsidesofthetable.com

Kara Swisher—All Things
Digital (@KaraSwisher)
BoomTown
www.kara.allthingsd.com

Bill Taylor (@PracticallyRad)
Practically Radical
www.blogs.harvardbusiness
.org/taylor/

Andrew Warner (@Mixergy)
Mixergy
www.mixergy.com

Noam Wasserman
(@NoamWass)
Noam Wasserman's "Founder
Frustrations" Blog
www.founderresearch.blogspot
.com

Fred Wilson (@FredWilson)
A VC
www.avc.com

PHOTO CREDITS

Photo of Quan Zhou on p. 200, provided by Quan Zhou

Photo of Henry Nguyen on p. 204, provided by Henry Nguyen

Photo of Irena Goldenberg on p. 214, provided by Irena
Goldenberg

Photo of Terry McGuire on p. 221, Bachrach Photography

INDEX